Ransomed, Redeemed, and Forgiven

Ransomed, Redeemed, and Forgiven

Money and the Atonement

David H. McIlroy

WIPF & STOCK · Eugene, Oregon

RANSOMED, REDEEMED, AND FORGIVEN
Money and the Atonement

Copyright © 2022 David H. McIlroy. All rights reserved. Except for brief quotations in critical publications or reviews, no part of this book may be reproduced in any manner without prior written permission from the publisher. Write: Permissions, Wipf and Stock Publishers, 199 W. 8th Ave., Suite 3, Eugene, OR 97401.

Wipf & Stock
An Imprint of Wipf and Stock Publishers
199 W. 8th Ave., Suite 3
Eugene, OR 97401

www.wipfandstock.com

PAPERBACK ISBN: 978-1-6667-3451-5
HARDCOVER ISBN: 978-1-6667-9043-6
EBOOK ISBN: 978-1-6667-9044-3

Unless otherwise indicated, Scripture quotations are taken from the Holy Bible, New International Version®, NIV®. Copyright © 1973, 1978, 1984, 2011 by Biblica, Inc.™ Used by permission of Zondervan. All rights reserved worldwide. www.zondervan.comThe "NIV" and "New International Version" are trademarks registered in the United States Patent and Trademark Office by Biblica, Inc.™

Scripture quotations marked (NASB) are taken from the (NASB®) New American Standard Bible®, Copyright © 1960, 1971, 1977, 1995, 2020 by The Lockman Foundation. Used by permission. All rights reserved. www.lockman.org"

Scripture quotations marked (CSB) have been taken from the Christian Standard Bible®, Copyright © 2017 by Holman Bible Publishers. Used by permission. Christian Standard Bible® and CSB® are federally registered trademarks of Holman Bible Publishers.

Lyrics from "Overwhelmed by Love" by Noel Richards. All rights reserved. Used by permission.

Lyrics from "In Christ Alone" by Keith Getty and Stuart Townend – Integrity Song #32172. Copyright: © 2001 Thankyou Music (Adm. by CapitolCMG-Publishing.com excl. UK & Europe, adm. at IntegrityRights.com). All rights reserved. Used by permission.

Lyrics from "Forgiven" by Craig and Phyllis Musseau – Integrity Song #50153. Copyright: © 1992 MERCY/VINEYARD PUBLISHING (ASCAP) & VINEYARD SONGS (CANADA) (SOCAN) (all adm at IntegrityRights.com). All rights reserved. Used by permission.

Lyrics from "I Will Offer Up My Life (This Thankful Heart)" by Matt Redman – Integrity Song #27232. Copyright: © 1994 Thankyou Music (Adm. by CapitolCMGPublishing.com excl. UK & Europe, Adm at IntegrityRights.com). All rights reserved. Used by permission.

Lyrics from "Turn Your Eyes" by George Romanacce, Kevin Winebarger, Nathan Stiff, Nic Trout, and Helen Howarth Lemmel – Integrity Song #22468. Copyright: © 2019 Sovereign Grace Praise/BMI (adm by Integrity's Praise! Music), Sovereign Grace Worship/ASCAP (adm by Integrity Worship Music), Sovereign Grace Songs/SESAC (adm by Integrity's Alleluia! Music), New Spring Publishing Inc. – CMG Song #216852. Copyright © 2019 New Spring Publishing Inc. (ASCAP) (adm. at CapitolCMGPublishing.com) All rights reserved. Used by permission.

Lyrics from "Amazing Grace (My Chains Are Gone)" by Chris Tomlin – CMG Song #40656. Copyright © 2006 worshiptogether.com Songs (ASCAP) sixsteps Music (ASCAP) Vamos Publishing (ASCAP) (adm. at CapitolCMGPublishing.com). All rights reserved. Used by permission.

Lyrics from "Lord I Lift Your Name On High" by Rick Founds – CMG Song #22747. Copyright © 1989 Universal Music - Brentwood Benson Publ. (ASCAP) (adm. at CapitolCMGPublishing.com). All rights reserved. Used by permission.

Lyrics from "Lord, for the Years" by Timothy Dudley-Smith. © in the USA and Canada 1969 Hope Publishing Company, Carol Stream, IL 60188. All rights reserved. Used by permission.

Lyrics from "Amazing Love (My Lord What Love Is This)" by Graham Kendrick. © 1989 Make Way Music (admin. by Music Services in the Western Hemisphere) All Rights Reserved. ASCAP. Used by permission.

Lyrics from "Before the Throne of God Above" (1867) by Charitie Lees Bancroft. Public domain.

Lyrics from "He Ransomed Me" (1916) by Julia H. Johnston. Public domain.

Lyrics from "Praise, my soul, the King of Heaven" (1834) by Henry Francis Lyte. Public domain.

Lyrics from "When I Survey The Wondrous Cross" (1707) by Isaac Watts. Public domain.

In memory of Rev. Dr. Joel Edwards, in gratitude for his example and his encouragement. His legacy is a debt I, and many others, will continue to pay forward in thankfulness, forgiveness, liberty and the pursuit of justice, freedom, and reconciliation.

Table of Contents

Introduction: Picturing the Unimaginable; Calculating the Incalculable 1

Ransom and the Power of Evil 18

Redemption and the Cost of Salvation 37

Forgiveness and the Debt to God 67

The Economy of Resurrection 94

Bibliography 121

Subject Index 127

Scripture Index 135

Introduction

Picturing the Unimaginable; Calculating the Incalculable

Why read this book?

THIS BOOK has a very simple aim: to open up what the Bible means when it talks about Jesus' death as a ransom, as redemption, and as forgiveness. Each of those terms has to do with money and with payment, both in their origin and as they would have been understood by those who first heard the good news about Jesus' death and resurrection.

This book is an adventure: an adventure of discovering the depth of meaning behind the images of ransom, redemption, and forgiveness. More than just finding out how the Bible uses pictures connected to money, I want us to discover together what it feels like to be ransomed, what it means to be redeemed, and what it is to experience forgiveness.

I have written this book for those people who have sat in churches and listened to preachers talking about redemption and forgiveness but who never had explained to them that these words were not originally religious words but words describing economic realities. I have also written this book for those who were vaguely aware that the ideas of ransom, redemption, and forgiveness have something to do with money, but who are unsure precisely how. Finally, I have written this book for those who have gotten themselves into debt, who have seen their goods, cars, and homes repossessed, or who have found themselves trapped by forces beyond their control. We sometimes say that people are "drowning in debt." Debt, like guilt, is something that can weigh us down and swallow us up.

I became interested in the way in which the Bible talks about money and connects money with the death of Jesus because of my day job as a barrister (the English equivalent of a trial attorney) dealing with court cases involving banks. The pictures of ransom, redemption, and forgiveness which the Bible uses are ones I recognize. I spend my time arguing in courts about money, payments, obligations, debts, and guarantees. I also teach banking law to university students, which gives me the opportunity to think more widely about patterns of debt and ways in which the law handles the consequences of debt. When I looked back through history and to the time of the Bible I discovered that earlier hearers of the good news about Jesus would have understood particular things when the ideas of ransom, redemption, and forgiveness were used. I suspect that the contemporary Western church has become so comfortable with thinking about ransom, redemption, and forgiveness as spiritual realities that we have lost sight of their original meaning as descriptions relating to money.

What I want to do in this book is to explore what it means today and what it meant in the time of the Bible to be ransomed from a kidnapper, to be redeemed from slavery, and to be forgiven from indebtedness. My hope is that as I do so this will enrich our understanding of what the Bible means when it describes Jesus' death and resurrection as the payment of a ransom, as our redemption from slavery, and as the forgiveness of our debt to God.

"The atonement" is how theologians describe the cross when they are exploring theories about its meaning. This book does not seek to develop a complete theory or model of the atonement. It is, instead, an invitation to join with me in using our imagination to put ourselves in the place of a kidnap victim in need of someone to

Introduction

pay the ransom, a debt-slave hoping for someone to pay the price for their redemption, and a hopeless, bankrupt debtor unable to pay what they owe to their creditors.

You already know the metaphors

The ideas of ransom, redemption, and forgiveness enjoy an important place in popular expressions of Christianity, at least measured in terms of the songs we sing. Both traditional hymns and newer songs refer to what Jesus has done in monetary terms. Jesus has ransomed us, he has paid the price, he has purchased us, he has paid our debt, he has forgiven us.

Chris Tomlin's 2006 updating of John Newton's great hymn, "Amazing Grace," adds the lyrics:

> My chains are gone
> I have been set free
> My God, my Savior has ransomed me

The first verse of Julia H. Johnston's 1916 hymn, "He Ransomed Me," declares:

> There's a sweet and blessed story
> Of the Christ who came from glory
> Just to rescue me from sin and misery;
> He in loving-kindness sought me
> And from sin and shame hath brought me—
> Hallelujah! Jesus ransomed me.

In the third verse she blends the images of redemption and ransom, saying:

> With His precious blood He bought me,
> When I knew Him not He sought me,
> And in love divine He ransomed me.

The idea that Christ paid my debt is central stage in Graham Kendrick's 1989 hymn, "Amazing Love":

> My Lord, what love is this
> That pays so dearly,

> That I, the guilty one,
> May go free!
> [Chorus] *Amazing love, O what sacrifice,*
> *The Son of God given for me.*
> *My debt He pays, and my death He dies,*
> *That I might live, that I might live.*

It is also prominent in Noel Richards' song "Overwhelmed by Love," containing the line, "all my debt he paid"; in "Lord I Lift Your Name on High," by Rick Founds, which declares that Jesus went "From the earth to the cross, My debt to pay"; and frequently in hymns by Stuart Townend.

Older generations will recognize the same sentiment in Charitie Lees Bancroft's 1867 hymn, "Before the Throne of God Above," which confidently declares, "Because the sinless Savior died, My sinful soul is counted free," and "One with my Lord, I cannot die; My soul is purchased by His blood."

The ideas of ransom and forgiveness are brought together in Henry Francis Lyte's hymn, "Praise, my soul, the King of heaven." The first verse continues:

> To his feet your tribute bring;
> Ransomed, healed, restored, forgiven,
> Who like you his praise should sing?
> Alleluia, alleluia!
> Praise the everlasting King.

The last verse of Craig and Phyllis Musseau's 1992 song, "Forgiven," declares:

> Father God, you've forgiven all my sins
> There's no need to repay you
> Father God, help me walk in what you've done
> Your love, your grace and your mercy
> Your great mercy.

Those are just a few examples of how often we use images connected with money when we sing about the death and resurrection of Jesus. But, if my own experience is anything to go by, we don't often hear those images explained in sermons and their original reference to money is rarely explored.

Why do we need to talk about money?

In spite of how often our hymns and songs use images related to money, there hasn't been much written by Christian theologians which focuses specifically on the relationship between money and the cross. There seem to be two reasons for this. One is that recent discussion of the atonement has focused on the propriety, wisdom, value, and/or dangers associated with the penal substitution metaphor for the atonement, or at least popular (mis-)understandings of it. The second is that the monetary metaphors for the atonement are felt to be problematic. In the seventeenth century, the money imagery used in the Bible was a favorite theme for theologians. Great minds like John Owen and Hugo Grotius battled with one another and with heretics such as Faustus Socinus about the calculation and effect of the price paid by Jesus Christ. In the course of their debates, the monetary metaphors were stretched beyond their breaking point.

As a result, theologians have, for many years, tended to sidestep the metaphors (or to roll them into other metaphors, so ransom is treated merely as an aspect of sacrifice and redemption and forgiveness merely as part of the model of penal substitutionary atonement). Undoubtedly the greatest contemporary discussion of the atonement is Fleming Rutledge's *The Crucifixion*, but, across its more than six hundred pages, the ideas of redemption and forgiveness in particular are only examined in passing.

If heresy is usually exaggerated truth, then even if there are difficulties with the metaphors of ransom, redemption, and forgiveness, there is probably something to be learned from exploring them.

As well as the imperative to understand what we mean when we sing about Christ paying the price, the importance of debt in our world today is another major reason for looking at how and what the Bible says about debt and its effects. The last thirty years have been years in which debt has become a preoccupation for those living with its consequences and for those trying to think about how to create a just and sustainable future for our planet and its people. In the years leading up to the millennium, the Jubilee 2000 campaign focused on the debts of developing nations (whose young citizens were liable to pay for the expenditure of the dictators who had ruled over their parents and grandparents). Until 2008, citizens in the West enjoyed access to easy credit, but the global financial crisis revealed the unsustainability of these debts and the financial speculation built upon them. Citizens in the West and their children found themselves obliged to take on the debts of the banks which their governments had deemed too big to fail. Debt had become "the central paradigm of the global economy" even before the coronavirus pandemic began in 2020.[1] The measures taken to fight the global pandemic of COVID-19 have multiplied the debts of nations and pushed the poorest further into debt. Unless there is debt forgiveness on a massive scale, we will have locked in increased inequality, unemployment, and misery for generations to come.

The weight of debt in our lives and on our consciences has led to an explosion in writings by professors about the way in which it has come to dominate our lives. David Graeber, *Debt: The First 5,000 Years* (2011), tells the story of how debt has been present throughout the history of human society but how the way we have thought about debt has changed over time. Italian academic Elettra Stimilli, *Debt and Guilt* (2015), writing in a country whose debts are nearly unpayable, has explored the cult of debt and how indebtedness has become a psychological trauma afflicting our age.

The way in which debt has come to dominate the news agenda and our lives has prompted Christians to think again about debt as a material as well as a spiritual reality. Aid agencies working in famine relief and development identified the large debts owed by African countries in particular as major obstacles to progress in health and education. Christian Aid and others identified the year 2000 as a symbolic moment for a debt jubilee. Peter Selby in

---

1. Stimilli, *Debt and Guilt*, 32.

Introduction

Grace and Mortgage (1997) started thinking about the connections between such a need and the message the church has to share.

Alongside a concern about international debt, the consequences of personal debt were brutally brought home to John Kirkby when his business failed. Discovering that his experience was being repeated by many who had lost their jobs, had suffered relationship breakdowns, or who had simply been seduced by the promises of "buy now, pay later," he established Christians Against Poverty in the UK. John Kirkby tells his story in *Nevertheless* (2003).

Debt is such an all-consuming and fast-moving phenomenon in our times that the publishers have issued new editions and translations of the books mentioned above. Debt has become a universal phenomenon, a constant preoccupation for our time.

The global financial crisis, which began in 2008, was caused by banks which had mistakenly assumed that they could make debt their servant. They had piled on debt, borrowing thirty or forty times the amount of capital they had, placing large bets in the casino of the markets, confident that there would always be someone somewhere who would be willing to lend to them so that they could continue to gamble. In some of my other writings I have tried to understand why banks took such risks and what would need to be done to prevent a banking crisis from destroying our economies in future.

The global financial crisis coincided with the publication of a book which brought debt back to the center of theological attention. Gary A. Anderson's *Sin: A History* (2009) argues persuasively that by the time of Jesus, debt was the predominant way in which Jewish culture thought about sin. He traces this through the later writings in the Old Testament, through religious documents outside the Bible (for example, the Dead Sea Scrolls), and in the New Testament itself. Nathan Eubank has followed up Anderson's work by looking at Matthew's Gospel in *Wages of Cross-Bearing and Debt of Sin: The Economy of Heaven in Matthew's Gospel* (2013). It should be no surprise that Matthew, a Jewish tax collector probably writing his Gospel for a primarily Jewish audience, would use images related to money when trying to explain what he had found in Jesus.

But, as yet, there has not been a book which has concentrated on how the message of the cross applies to those of us experiencing the weight of debt in our time. This book seeks to fill that gap.

Pictures not diagrams

The images of ransom, redemption, and forgiveness are word-pictures; they are metaphors. Alastair Roberts and Andrew Wilson say, "metaphors have great power to fashion the way we conceptualize things ... If a ... metaphor is chosen well, it has the capacity to illuminate new worlds of meaning and help us see all sorts of connections we might otherwise have missed."[2]

A metaphor is a way of explaining something by comparing it to something else. Metaphors carry across part of what we picture when we think about one thing familiar to us to what we imagine when we think about something else (the word *metaphor* comes from the Greek words *meta*, meaning "across," and *pherein*, meaning "to carry"). The way metaphors work is that they introduce a new idea that the author wants to explain and they compare it with something which the audience is familiar with. (In case you are interested, the technical name for the familiar idea is the "explicans" and the name for the idea being introduced is the "explicandum.")

Metaphors and parables

N. T. Wright calls metaphors "mini-stories."[3] If metaphors are mini-stories, parables are extended metaphors. Some of Jesus' parables have just one central meaning. The parable of the pearl of great price is one of a number of parables in which Jesus is telling his listeners that the Kingdom of God is more valuable than

---

2. Roberts and Wilson, *Echoes of Exodus*, 23.
3. Wright, *New Testament*, 129.

INTRODUCTION

anything else in the world, and that it is worth giving up everything else in order to enjoy it.

Other parables have more depth. In the parable of the prodigal son, although the central dynamic is the relationship between the generous father and the prodigal son, Jesus also wants his religious listeners to see themselves in the figure of the crabbed, resentful brother who is not prepared to enjoy the reconciliation between his father and his scandalous younger brother. Even here, though, we go astray if we seek to impose meaning on every detail in the story. Can we really suppose, for example, that Jesus meant something specific when referring to the "pods that the pigs were eating" (Luke 15:16) beyond showing how tasteless and unsatisfying a life lived without God eventually becomes?

Jesus taught about the character of God in parables because he knew that these stories would help us understand more about who our loving Father is than any dictionary definition or philosophical arguments would do.[4] In the same way, we need stories, more than we need logical arguments, in order to begin to understand what it means to talk about God's love, wrath, justice, and mercy.[5]

This is particularly true when we think about the cross because, as Steve Holmes explains:

> The event of Calvary is unique. It is not just once in a series of similar acts of inspirational self-sacrifice, nor is it an example of a more general principle of law in operation. Rather the cross is so fundamental to any properly Christian account of relationship, justice, love, and a host of other human experiences that it cannot be described exhaustively in these ways. We just do not know what self-sacrifice means until we see Jesus on the cross. The same is true of justice. If we think we know what self-sacrifice is, or what justice is, or whatever, and then force the cross to fit our understanding, we end up getting things the wrong way up; instead, we need to realize that we will

---

4. Holmes, *The Wondrous Cross*, 79.
5. Holmes, *The Wondrous Cross*, 6.

understand these things only when we understand them through the cross.[6]

Each of Jesus' original listeners and the people in the lands where the apostles evangelized would have immediately identified with the experiences of themselves or someone they knew when the words ransom, redemption, and forgiveness were used.

But metaphors don't work if the audience doesn't recognize the thing the author is using as the basis for the comparison. For example, a number of times the Bible mentions snow. Twice in the Hebrew Scriptures someone suffering from a skin disease is said to have skin "as white as snow" (Num 12:10; 2 Kgs 5:27). After his adultery with Bathsheba, King David prayed that he would be washed "whiter than snow" (Ps 51:7; see Isa 1:18). That image worked in Hebrew because the ancient Israelites were familiar with Mount Zalmon being covered in snow (Ps 68:14) and with snow in the mountains of Lebanon (Jer 18:14) (Jerusalem experienced heavy snowfall in 1950 and again in 2013). If you are trying to communicate the same idea to people who have never seen or heard of snow, you have to use a different image instead. Instead of saying that something is "as white as snow," it can be described as "as white as wool" or "as white as egret feathers."

Metaphors and their limits

A metaphor is a word-picture in which something is described by comparing it with something else. Metaphors are especially helpful in enabling us to imagine or understand or remember. A good metaphor communicates a single idea.

Two of the most famous word-pictures in the English language were written by the poets Robert Burns and William Wordsworth. Robert Burns updated the words of the folk song "My Love Is Like a Red, Red Rose," while William Wordsworth began his poem "Daffodils" with the metaphor, "I wandered lonely as a cloud."

---

6. Holmes, *The Wondrous Cross*, 7–8.

Introduction

Those of you who were paying attention during grammar lessons at school will want to point out that both of these figures of speech are, technically, *similes*, because the comparison is made using the words "like" and "as." Similes say that one thing is *like* another. Metaphors are more audacious; they say that one thing *is* another. (I used to get frustrated when listening to preachers or reading theologians who would say that *x* is, "in a sense" or "in a certain sense," "in a real sense," or, worst of all, "in a very real sense," *y*. I now understand that what these speakers and writers were doing was creating stopping points between the bare comparison of a simile on the one hand and the daring identification of the qualities of one thing with the qualities of another made in an unqualified metaphor.) Grammar lesson over. Metaphors and similes both belong to the field of picture language and, for the remainder of this book, I will refer simply to metaphors.

We were, before the grammar lesson, talking about the poets Burns and Wordsworth, and their pictures of love like a red rose and of wandering lonely as a cloud. What's the central idea those two metaphors convey? When Burns says, "My love is like a red, red rose," he is drawing on some of the key characteristics of roses: their beauty and their smell. He is saying that the beauty and the fragrance of his love are similar to the beauty and fragrance of a fresh rose with a deep red color. He is trying to explain that his love was as beautiful as a red rose, and he felt similar feelings when looking at her as when he looked at a red rose. When Wordsworth said he wandered lonely as a cloud, it was the constant movement of the clouds and the fact that they are far away from other human beings that were the central ideas he was drawing out.

The same is true of the metaphors used in the Bible. When Psalm 23 tells us, "The Lord is my shepherd," it does not mean that God is a poor man who sleeps outdoors and smells of sheep. As Hans Boersma points out, "Not all aspects of shepherds are transferable to God,"[7] but some are. The metaphor of God as shepherd is, as Psalm 23 goes on to explore, about how God loves, protects, and cares for us like a good shepherd looks after his sheep.

7. Boersma, *Violence, Hospitality and the Cross*, 101.

All metaphors break down at some stage. When we use a metaphor we are drawing a line between some, but not all, features of two different things. The more different the two things being compared using the metaphor, the more likely they are to break down.

We can see this if we think again about Burns's poem about his love being like a red, red rose. As well as their beauty and fragrance, another key characteristic of roses are their thorns. If someone had asked Robert Burns whether he meant that his love had thorns like a rose, or that she had a prickly personality and could cut you if you were not careful, the poet would have said, "Of course not."

And as for Wordsworth's lonely clouds, anyone who looks up into the sky knows that sometimes there is just a single cloud in the clear blue sky and at other times there are lots of clouds moving across the sky together. The reason why Wordsworth can wander as lonely as a cloud is because clouds are remote from human beings.

So P. T. Forsyth warns about the limits of metaphors: Words and metaphors, if we attempt to "stretch [them] to the measure of eternal things," will break under us.[8]

Picturing the unimaginable

The death and resurrection of Jesus Christ were, together with the incarnation, the defining moments of human history. Everything else has to be understood in terms of them. As Hans Boersma says, "Every other temporal event that takes place in . . . human history . . . derives its being and significance from the great Christ event itself."[9] Theories and descriptions can help us to appreciate some of the truth of what occurred when Jesus died on the cross and was raised again to life by the Father. But the magnitude of the events is bigger than any explanation of them that we can offer. None of our ideas, no matter how indispensable they may be as a

---

8. Forsyth, *The Work of Christ*, 210.
9. Boersma, *Heavenly Participation*, 127.

Introduction

way of coming to terms with the events of Easter, can exhaust the meaning of the death and resurrection of the Son of God.

Because there is no other event which even falls into the same category as the death and resurrection of Jesus Christ, we can only use analogies or metaphors to try to understand it. We can say that the effect of the death of Christ for us is *like* being ransomed from a kidnapper; is *like* being forgiven an enormous, unpayable debt; is *like* being bought back from slavery—but in every respect what God has done for us in Christ is bigger than any human experience of paying a ransom, being forgiven a debt, or being freed from slavery. These word-pictures are like miniature paintings of an event bigger than the biggest sports final, political rally, or war-defining battle. The things that seem so real and tangible to us are, as C. S. Lewis reminds us, just shadows of the fullness of what God has done.[10] There are colors, shapes, and textures to our salvation which we have yet to begin discovering. This is really important. Jesus' death and resurrection is the reality of which the word-pictures of ransom, redemption, and forgiveness help us to glimpse a part. We must not mistake them for the reality any more than we should mistake Monet's paintings for the ever-changing beauty of the flowers in the garden at Giverny.

If the metaphors don't make sense, if we don't find them helpful, that isn't too much of a problem. I can drive a car successfully even though I have no idea of how an internal combustion engine or electronics really work. In the same way, we are saved if we put our trust in Jesus and in what his death and resurrection achieved for us whether we understand how he did it or not. C. S. Lewis put it well when he said, "Theories about Christ's death are not Christianity: they are explanations about how it works."[11]

Nonetheless, because the experiences of being ransomed, being redeemed, and being forgiven are experiences with which we can identify, they can help us to understand more of what it is like to have been saved by the Incarnation, Death and Resurrection of Jesus Christ, Son of God, Son of Mary.

10. Lewis, *The Last Battle*, 173.
11. Lewis, *Mere Christianity*, 54.

The biblical basis for monetary metaphors for the atonement

The monetary metaphors for the atonement have a sound biblical basis. They are rooted in the Hebrew Scriptures, present in the Gospels, and used by the writers of the New Testament letters.

The metaphors in the Old Testament

The idea of redemption is a central theme of Leviticus 25 and 27 and is mentioned in many other passages in the Pentateuch. In Leviticus 27, the idea is of a person owing something as a sacrifice to God. Various passages in Exodus, Leviticus, and Numbers talk about a person paying a ransom for their life (Exod 30:12; Lev 27:29; Num 35:31–32). The importance of forgiveness is a constant theme in the Old Testament, with nearly sixty references. At the very beginning of the story of Israel, Joseph's brothers, recognizing that their treatment of him years before meant that their lives were in his hands, beg him "to forgive your brothers their sins and the wrongs they committed in treating you so badly" (Gen 50:17). The references throughout the Old Testament thereafter are always to the forgiveness of sins (e.g. Ps 79:9), offences (e.g. Job 7:20), transgressions (e.g. Ps 32:1), iniquity (e.g. Ps 25:1), wickedness (e.g. Exod 34:9), rebellion (e.g. Exod 23:21), fault (Ps 19:12), and guilt (Lev 6:7). Although forgiveness is already being used as a metaphor in the Old Testament, as we shall see, the connection between guilt and debt is very close indeed.

The metaphors in the New Testament

In the Gospels, Jesus taught his disciples to pray for the *forgiveness* of their debts in the Lord's Prayer (in Matt 6:12 and Luke 11:4). He taught about human beings' relationship to God and to one another by telling a parable about an unmerciful servant who experienced forgiveness from an unpayable debt yet failed to forgive someone who owed him a much smaller sum (Matt 18:23–35).

INTRODUCTION

In Matthew 20:28, talking about himself, Jesus declared that "the Son of Man did not come to be served, but to serve, and to give his life as a ransom for many." In Luke 21:28, predicting the events that would happen before his return, Jesus told his disciples, "When these things take place, stand up and lift your heads, because your redemption is drawing near."

In the New Testament letters, Paul writes about forgiveness and redemption to the Romans (Rom 3:24; 4:7; 8:23), the Corinthians (1 Cor 1:30; 2 Cor 2), the Ephesians (Eph 1:7, 14; 4:30) and the Colossians (Col 1:14; 3:13). The writer of the Letter to the Hebrews explores the link between sacrifice and forgiveness (Heb 8:12; 9:22; 10:18), while John stresses forgiveness in 1 John 1:9 and 2:12. Both 1 Timothy 2:6 and Hebrews 9:15 describe Jesus' death as a ransom.

Metaphors which overlap

The metaphors of ransom, redemption, and forgiveness are like the interlocking circles in a Venn diagram. They run into one another. The metaphors for ransom and redemption are particularly close. They share the same root (*lutrosis*) in Greek. In Hebrew, there are three words which cover their semantic range: the verbs *padah* and *kipper* and the noun *go'el*. *Padah* is associated with the idea of winning a victory, *kipper* with the idea of paying a price or making a sacrifice (particularly of the Passover lamb), and a *go'el* is a kinsman-redeemer, the one who has reason to win a victory, pay a price, or make a sacrifice in order to free a relative from captivity.

As we shall see, translating *padah* into English as "to ransom" captures its focus on the effectiveness of our liberation, whilst translating *kipper* as "to redeem" and its related noun *kopher* as "redemption" places the emphasis on the cost of redemption. *Go'el*, in turn, draws our attention to the person who is coming to rescue us and to his relationship to us.

When we listen to a piece of music, we can concentrate on what the violins are playing, or the sounds of the horns, or the noise of the percussion instruments, but each of them is contributing to the overall beauty of the piece. In a similar way, although we will discover particular things by focusing on each of the monetary metaphors in turn, they are not separate or discordant images but part of a glorious, harmonious overall picture.

Hebrews 9 brings the three metaphors together. Verse 12 tells us that Jesus "entered the Most Holy Place once for all by his own blood, thus obtaining eternal redemption [*lutrosis*]," verse 15 that "For this reason Christ is the mediator of a new covenant, that those who are called may receive the promised eternal inheritance—now that he has died as a ransom [*apolutrosis*] to set them free from the sins committed under the first covenant," and verse 22 that "the law [of Moses] requires that nearly everything be cleansed with blood, and without the shedding of blood there is no forgiveness [*aphesis*]."

Hebrews 9 shows how ransom and redemption are not two separate concepts in the time of the New Testament. The Greek word for "ransom" is formed by adding the prefix *apo-* to the word for redemption. A *lutrosis* is the act of paying the full price (*lutron*) to release a slave. An *apolutrosis* is the release effected by a *lutron*. Because we have been ransomed, we are redeemed.

What to expect in the rest of this book

Metaphors enable us to make leaps of imagination. They help us to think of electricity as a current and of light as a wave. The first thing a good metaphor does is to catch our imagination. Once we have made the leap, then we can explore the new field of reference. For this reason, each chapter in this book will begin with a series of stories. I hope that one or more of the stories will help you to make the leap of imagination; to begin to sense what being ransomed, being redeemed, or being forgiven *feel like*. After the stories, I will explain a bit about the meaning of ransom, redemption, and forgiveness in financial transactions: why a ransom needs to be paid, what redemption means, what forgiveness really is all about. Once we have looked at that together, we will turn to how the Bible uses the images of ransom, redemption, and forgiveness—in the

INTRODUCTION

hope that what we have already seen will help us understand more deeply the ways in which the salvation Jesus has achieved is like the payment of a ransom, the redemption of a slave, or the forgiveness of a debtor.

Conclusion

This book does not pretend to be a complete theology of the atonement. Not even Fleming Rutledge's six-hundred-page book, *The Crucifixion: Understanding the Death of Jesus Christ*, is that. Instead, this book is an exploration of some word-pictures which have much more to show us than we might expect.

We sing about being ransomed, redeemed, and forgiven, but we don't often think too deeply about where these ideas come from and why the apostles use them so often in their attempt to explain the significance of Jesus' death and resurrection. Ransom, redemption, and forgiveness are all realities in the Old Testament and throughout history. Our world today is saturated with debt. Oppression, bankruptcy, debt-slavery, and kidnappings still occur on a horrific scale. In such a world, knowing that we have been ransomed, redeemed, and forgiven must lead us to act to rescue those who are captives, enslaved, and bankrupt, either spiritually or materially.

When thinking about the cross, the ideas of ransom, redemption, and forgiveness are pictures, not diagrams, shafts of light showing part of the effect and implications of the central events in human history, the atonement. They are not the only things to be said about the cross, they are not the only way of thinking about it, they are true but not the whole truth. What this book aims to do is not so much to help you to understand the cross fully but fully to stand under the cross; to deepen your sense of the enormous, incalculable lengths to which God was willing to go in order to rescue those who are unable to help themselves.

Ransom and the Power of Evil

What is it like to be kidnapped?

Paul and Rachel Chandler's story

IN OCTOBER 2009 the middle-aged British couple Paul and Rachel Chandler set sail from the Seychelles Islands in the Indian Ocean to travel to Tanzania in Africa. Ninety miles offshore, their small yacht was boarded by armed pirates from Somalia, who held them hostage on land for more than a year, demanding a ransom of many millions of dollars. The British government stood by its policy of refusing to pay.

What must it have felt like to the Chandlers, to be trapped, separated, alone, helpless, hungry, desperate? They spent over a year in captivity, some in solitary confinement and most in makeshift desert camps, guarded by young men carrying AK-47 assault rifles and often high on drugs. How did they cope with the boredom, the constant threat of violence, the fear of death? If you want to find out, you can read the book they have written called *Hostage: A Year at Gunpoint with Somali Gangsters*. At the heart of the experience of being a hostage is the realization that you are helpless, that there is nothing else you can do to get out.

So, what happened to the Chandlers? First, their extended family entered into negotiations with the kidnappers. The kidnappers started off by demanding $7 million, but the negotiators talked them down to $440,000. The money was raised and dropped in cash from an airplane in June 2010, but Paul and Rachel Chandler were still not freed. By then, the kidnappers had been encouraged to hold out for more by stories in the media that other parties might also pay to set the Chandlers free. After almost five more months, their release was finally negotiated by a Somali taxi driver from East London, so ashamed by his countrymen's crime that he raised a further $200,000 from Somalis in Britain and personally delivered it to the kidnappers in exchange for the hostages.

Imagine how the Chandlers felt as they experienced freedom for the first time. Was the horror of their imprisonment outweighed by the joy of their release?

Sahil Saeed's story

In 2010, Sahil Saeed, a five-year-old boy from Oldham in England, was visiting his grandmother in Pakistan. On March 4, 2010, gunmen burst into his grandmother's house and kidnapped Sahil. He was taken to a room without a bed, given nothing but rice to eat, and told that if he did not co-operate the kidnappers would fit him with an explosives jacket and "blow him to pieces."

Two days later, the kidnappers telephoned Sahil's father, demanding a ransom of £100,000. Friends and relatives of the family in Oldham helped to raise the ransom, many using their savings or selling family gold and jewelry in order to help. Sahil's uncle travelled to Paris where, watched by French undercover police, he handed over the money to the kidnappers.

The police followed the kidnappers through France and into Spain before the news came that Sahil had been released. He had been dumped on a roadside in the middle of nowhere, but was recognized by a passerby who had seen TV reports of the case, and he was taken to safety.

Spanish police then stepped in, arresting the organizers of the kidnap, a Pakistani man called Muhammad Zahid Saleem and his Romanian wife, Gianina Monica Neruja. Both were sentenced to ten years in prison by a Spanish court.

The power of evil

The big idea at the heart of the ransom metaphor is the power of evil. The Somali pirates had no rights over Paul and Rachel Chandler, the kidnappers of Sahil had no rights over him: what they had was power—violent, intimidating, death-dealing power. We are all subject to powers which enslave through coercion and deception. As P. T. Forsyth wrote in 1938, "We have to deal with a world in a bondage it could not break."[1]

All of us are trapped by the forces of evil, sin, selfishness, and death; by forces beyond our control, beyond our understanding, and often invisible to us. You can't be rescued unless you admit that you are trapped. You won't be rescued unless you are prepared to call out for help. The challenge of the cross is to look long and hard at our lives and to see where we are held hostage by our own self-centeredness and by our complicity in world-systems which oppress both others and ourselves.

The Bible and theology describe the powers of evil in various ways. One list warns against the world, the flesh, and the devil; another against the dangers of money, sex, and power. The first list refers to three battles we face. The devil represents out-and-out evil. There are, at work in our world, forces which seek to destroy and to dominate. Anyone who doubts that needs to get out more! The flesh refers to our natural appetites and desires, which we need to keep under control lest greed make our bodies too fat or our sex drives make a mess of our personal relationships. The world describes the world's value system, those prizes of reputation, status, and influence which we chase after. My own profession offers a number of these: the prestige of being a Supreme Court judge, the status of being a Senior Partner or a QC, and the luxury cars, second homes, and fine wines lawyers can aspire to afford.

The trio of money, sex, and power refers to things which, though good in themselves, can corrupt us in an instant or gradually over time. Power becomes a need to dominate; sex becomes a

---

1. Forsyth, *The Work of Christ*, 110.

gratification in itself rather than an expression of intimacy; money turns into mammon, an end in itself rather than a tool.

Jesus identifies money as one of the powers which hold human beings captive. Money as an object of worship, money as an end in itself, money as a pitiless, unforgiving master is personified as "mammon." Mammon is the love of money which 1 Timothy 6:10 describes as *a* root of all kinds of evil. Mammon, and the security it offers, is deceitful and seductive, which is why it is so hard for those who (like many lawyers such as myself) have money to escape its attractions and demands (Matt 19:24). It is mammon which holds the man in Luke 18:18 captive. Luke refers to him as a "ruler." His wealth has brought him both status and security. Although the rich young man can say with a straight face that he has not broken any of the Ten Commandments, his heart is enthralled by his possessions.

The Bible recognizes how the powers corrupt institutions and individuals. We need saving from the powers, but also from those (such as the pirates, the bankers, the lawyers, the brothel keepers, and all the rest of us) who have become their instruments.

Our decisions to choose to co-operate with and to succumb to mammon or to any of these forces of evil the Bible calls sin. And sin leads to death. James 1:15 explains the process: "After desire has conceived, it gives birth to sin; and sin, when it is full-grown, gives birth to death." Death is the consequence of sin; it is the payment for it. It is for this reason, Vladimir Lossky tells us that "the Son of God came down from heaven to accomplish the work of our salvation, to liberate us from the captivity of the devil, to destroy the dominion of sin in our nature, and to undo death, which is the wages of sin."[2]

Edmund and the White Witch

C. S. Lewis gives us a vivid picture of how we are all captivated by evil. In *The Lion, the Witch and the Wardrobe* (a book translated

---

2. Lossky, *In the Image and Likeness of God*, 98.

into forty-seven languages), he describes how Edmund comes into the magical land of Narnia, where he meets the evil White Witch. Edmund is seduced by the White Witch's promises of pleasure and power, but he does not know what he is letting himself in for. The White Witch tempts him with Turkish delight, and once he has become addicted, she treats him as her slave.

Edmund is promised, if he delivers his sisters and brother into the White Witch's hands, that he will be a prince, wearing a gold crown and eating Turkish delight all day long. His reward for his betrayal of Peter, Susan, and Lucy is, instead, nothing but dry bread and water and a beating.

When C. S. Lewis wanted to explain what led Jesus to die on the cross, he used the imagery of ransom. In order to free Edmund, Aslan, the great lion who is the true ruler of Narnia, agrees to be exchanged for Edmund. A hostage exchange takes place, in which the true king surrenders himself to the usurper in order to free the traitor Edmund. Now apparently in the White Witch's power, Aslan is shaved, humiliated, and then killed at a place called the Stone Table.

Our addiction to evil

Those who are at the bottom of the social pile, who have lost jobs or been forced to carry on work in dangerous conditions during the COVID-19 pandemic, know that they are the victims of powers beyond their control. For those who have done well in the lottery of life, there is a constant temptation to believe that we are largely free from the effects of the powers, that it is only others who are oppressed or used by them.

Timothy Dudley-Smith's hymn "Lord, for the Years" attempts to puncture this sense of self-satisfaction. The lyric "spirits oppressed by pleasure, wealth, and care" is striking. Despite the fact that many in the West have more money, more security, and more opportunities for leisure (except when a global pandemic strikes) than the overwhelming majority of humanity has ever had, our pursuit of these things has left us stressed, anxious, and unhappy.

The word "addiction" has its origins in a legal process for dealing with unpaid debts. In her book *Debt and Guilt*, Elettra Stimilli explains how in the Twelve Tables, the earliest recorded Roman laws, "if the debtor did not return the due sum by the deadline, the creditor could tie him and take him with him. He became *addictus*, that is, he underwent the executive procedure of *addictio*, though which he was at the total and material disposal of the other... The creditor could carry the debtor with him, tie him for sixty days and present him on the market for sale. If no buyers were found, the creditor could sell the debtor abroad or kill him."[3] That process of *addictio*, in which one person becomes totally under the control of another, is where the word "addiction" comes from.

The West's relentless optimism of the nineteenth century has been replaced by fears about a dystopian future. In *1984*, George Orwell predicted in a future in which external forces (spies, prisons, torture chambers, the state) would destroy our freedom. In contrast, Aldous Huxley in *Brave New World* thought that our freedom would be destroyed by enemies within (innate desires, egotism, hedonism, leisure). The assessment of Neil Postman is that Huxley, not Orwell, was proved right in the long run.[4]

Roberts and Wilson agree with Neil Postman's conclusion. They point to how Suzanne Collins's *The Hunger Games* show us is that "the fatuous, green-haired, celebrity-obsessed crowds in the Capitol are in many ways more captive, less free, and more pitiable than the bread-starved vagrants in District 12. Their chains are invisible, but they are no less enslaved."[5] Systems can trap us even more effectively through our desires than through our fears.

Paul and Rachel Chandler and Sahil Saeed experienced physical captivity, but the Bible's message is that none of us is free. Each of our souls is in captivity to the powers of evil. Human beings are victims of powers that we cannot control with which we have

---

3. Stimilli, *Debt and Guilt*, 36–37.
4. Postman, *Amusing Ourselves to Death*.
5. Roberts and Wilson, *Echoes of Exodus*, 51.

surrendered, collaborated, or come to terms. The alcoholic knows this: "First you take a drink, then the drink takes a drink, then the drink takes you." Addiction begins by making bad choices but it does not end there.

Moreover, although each of us needs to take our own guilt with the utmost seriousness, there is more to sin than just individual responsibility. As a white Anglo-Irish male, I am heir to a legacy in which my country has benefited from the slave trade and from its oppression of and disregard for the people of Ireland. My lifestyle is subsidized by structures of international trade which are skewed in favor of the imperial powers and against those countries that they subjugated.

We cannot earn our own escape

The ransom metaphor therefore tells us that salvation is wholly different from drawing up a balance sheet at the end of a person's life. The ancient Egyptians believed that, after a person's death, their heart was weighed on a set of scales. Only if their heart weighed less than a feather would they pass on to eternal life. The idea that the eternal destiny of human beings is to be measured on a set of scales and depends on our good deeds outweighing our bad deeds is as mistaken as it is persistent. The ransom metaphor (and, as we shall see, the idea of forgiveness) is completely incompatible with any suggestion that our eternal destiny is a matter of setting our good and our bad deeds off against one another. There have been many such attempts, including Cosimo de Medici's backing for the construction of the enormous brick dome on the cathedral in Florence (still the largest brick built dome in the world, six hundred years later). This and any other endowment to a church by a merchant or king was a bad bargain if it was an attempt to purchase an indulgence for their sins. God is not a prostitute who wants our money; God is a lover who wants our hearts and our whole selves.

But, if no one can release themselves from our captivity to the powers of evil, it is equally true that no one is too far in thrall to those powers to be beyond rescue. Ours is a culture in which two lies are present: one is the lie that if only we believe in ourselves enough we can save ourselves; the other is the lie that our destiny is fixed and that no one can rescue us.

The picture of Jesus' death as a ransom teaches us is that the rescue mission was for all men and women. Jesus didn't just die for the good people, the kind people, the nice people. Jesus didn't just die for the ones who are okay. He died for the nasty people, the horrible people, the messed-up people, the confused people, the desperate people. Jesus didn't just die for you and me and for the Chandlers. He also died for the hostage takers, the people traffickers, and the slave masters.

It is not enough to believe in yourself

The main point of the ransom metaphor is to emphasize that human beings are trapped. We are being held captive by the forces of evil. We are powerless to break free from the evil which ensnares us, both the evil which we think and do and the evil which others inflict on us. Like the Chandlers and like Sahil Saheed, we are entirely at the mercy of our captor. Like them, we have no chance of paying the ransom money ourselves. Someone else had to do that on our behalf.

Because we are captives, the Bible recognizes that it is not enough to "believe in yourself." In the end, none of us is strong enough to succeed on our own. Whether it is because of our failures, shortcomings, or poor choices on the one hand or through circumstances on the other, we will find ourselves in situations from which we cannot rescue ourselves. This is deeply countercultural, cutting across the message of many contemporary songs, musicals, and films. Our culture encourages each of us to "be your own hero." Jeremiah 17:5 warns, "Cursed is the one who trusts in human beings, who depends on flesh for his strength and whose heart turns away from the Lord."

We cannot buy our way out of sin or into a relationship with God. This is glorious, good news for those who have nothing to bargain with, but a challenge to those who think that their wealth, good works, or religious observance will enable them to come to some sort of arrangement with God.

When it comes to the debt we have incurred by sinning, the Old Testament cannot think of anyone who has enough credit with God to be able to save not only themselves but others. Psalm 49:7–9 says, "No man can redeem the life of another or give to God a ransom for him—the ransom for a life is costly, no payment is ever enough—that he should live for ever and not see decay."

In Ezekiel 14, God lists four judgments that he will send against Jerusalem: war and famine and wild beasts and plague. As each judgment is listed, God says that even if Noah, Daniel, and Job were alive at the time the judgment fell, "they alone would be saved" (Ezek 14:16). In his analysis, T. F. Torrance says, "In the ultimate things in man's relation with God, in judgment in death, in disaster, no one can be a *go'el* [kinsman-redeemer] for a fellow human being. God alone can step in and deliver us and bestow life upon us in redemption."[6] What makes Jesus unique is that he, as one who is both the Son of God and the only human being to have lived in perfect covenant-faithfulness with God the Father, is able to give his life as a ransom (*lutron*) for many (Mark 10:45, 1 Tim 2:6).

You cannot be ransomed unless you recognize that you are a captive. You cannot be redeemed unless you admit that you are enslaved. It is precisely when we accept that we are trapped in patterns of wrongdoing and that we are too weak to free ourselves that God is able to come into our lives to rescue us. Isaiah 59:20 promises that "The Redeemer will come to Zion, to those in Jacob who repent of their sins." Have you ever felt totally overwhelmed, completely insignificant, and utterly unable to see a way out? Isaiah 41:14 reads, "'Do not be afraid, O worm Jacob, O little Israel, for I myself will help you,' declares the LORD, your Redeemer, the Holy One of Israel."

---

6. Torrance, *Atonement*, 47.

Jesus' death as a ransom

In order for the Chandlers to be freed, someone had to pay a ransom. They were powerless to escape the grip of the pirates who had kidnapped them. Those who have been kidnapped, enslaved, or taken hostage cannot free themselves. They need someone to pay the price of their rescue.

In Matthew 20:28, talking about himself, Jesus declares that "the Son of Man did not come to be served, but to serve, and to give his life as a ransom [*lutron*] for many." Jesus was not using the term *lutron* merely as a figure of speech. Outside of the Bible, *lutron* was the term used to describe "the sum paid for the manumission of a slave, or the redemption of a pledge, or for the release of a prisoner of war."[7] In the Septaguint, the Greek translation of the Old Testament, *lutron* was used to refer to the money paid to redeem slaves (Lev 19:20; 25:51–52; Isa 45:13) as well as to the payments to redeem the firstborn of Israel (Num 3:12, 46–51; 18:15). A ransom *(lutron)* was, in both the Bible read to Jesus' listeners and in the world around them, a payment of money. *Lutron* is used in the same way in the New Testament, particularly in Matthew's Gospel. Nathan Eubank is insistent that *lutron*, the Greek word for "ransom," always refers in the Bible to some price or exchange and never simply to rescuing or delivering in general terms.[8] Although the verb form can have a more general reference, when the noun *lutron* itself is used, it is always talking about payment.

So, when Matthew 20:28 says the Son of Man gave his life as a ransom for many, Matthew means that Jesus made a payment sufficient to secure the release of many from captivity. As Steve Holmes explains:

> In the Bible, *ransom* is used more than once to describe the price that must be paid to set someone free from their sins and from the threat of hell. Job 33:24 comes in the middle of a long passage where Elihu imagines the fate of people who have sinned (verse 27), who need "a

---

7. Torrance, *Atonement*, 172.
8. Eubank, *Wages of Cross-Bearing*, 150–51.

mediator," who can say, "Deliver him from the Pit, for I have found a ransom" (verse 24). Psalm 49 asks what ransom price could possibly be enough for a person's life (verses 5–9), using this to mock those who trust in their wealth rather than in God. The psalmist goes on to announce that "God will ransom my soul from the power of the Pit—he will receive me" (verse 15). When Jesus said he would give his life "as a ransom for many," this notion of paying the unimaginably costly price necessary to rescue humanity must be what he meant.[9]

The king's ransom: Richard I

The phrase "a king's ransom" is used to describe something that is incredibly expensive. The people of England once had to pay such a ransom in order to secure the release of Richard I "the Lionheart."

The legend of Robin Hood is set against the backdrop of bad King John and good King Richard. King Richard is out of the country. In his absence, his brother John (aided and abetted by his henchman, the Sheriff of Nottingham) has usurped the throne and is oppressing the people through excessive taxation.

Told in those terms, the legend has all the romance of a story about the return of the true king (the same motif as in all the stories about Arthur or another king coming again or in Tolkien's *Lord of the Rings*). Unfortunately, the reality is somewhat more complex. King John was certainly bad; but King Richard was hardly good for the people of England. Richard loved his lands in France far more than England, and enjoyed fighting in the Crusades more than governing his subjects on either side of the Channel. In his ten-year reign, Richard may have spent as little as six months in England.

After his score-draw with Saladin in the Holy Land, Richard was shipwrecked and had to continue his journey by land. Just before Christmas in 1192, Richard was captured near Vienna by Duke Leopold of Austria. Richard remained imprisoned for over a

---

9. Holmes, *The Wondrous Cross*, 35.

year, until his ransom of 150,000 marks (100,000 pounds of silver) was paid. The cost of this king's ransom was paid by his mother, Eleanor, organizing taxation of both the church and the people to the level of one quarter of the value of their property. For all his bravura on the battlefield, Richard found himself a helpless captive, whose only hope was that his ransom would be paid from outside.

The king's ransom: Jesus' death

In Homer's poems in ancient Greece, prisoners of war became, and remained, slaves until they were ransomed by relatives or friends. In ancient Rome, whose wars were fought further afield, the relatives or friends of an enslaved prisoner of war had far less chance of knowing who to pay the ransom to. In 146 BC, when Carthage in North Africa was defeated, 55,000 of its inhabitants were taken into slavery.

In ancient Rome, a rich man or ruler could demonstrate their generosity and their greatness through an act of liberation. It was common for a rich man to include in his will provisions emancipating those slaves who had served him faithfully. Fears about mass emancipations becoming fashionable appear to have been behind the *Lex Fufia Caninia* (2 BC), which limited the number of slaves a master could emancipate in his will at one hundred.

Therefore, as Douglas Webster explains, "In the minds of [Paul's] original readers, the idea of a redeemer would conjure up a picture of a great benefactor liberating prisoners of war or emancipating slaves, even, if necessary, by paying some ransom price for them. This, says St. Paul, is what Christ has done for men through his Cross. He has set them free from bondage to sin."[10]

Rulers were supposed to rescue their people from oppression. Richard I's subjects in England and France ended up having to pay a king's ransom to rescue him. In contrast, Jesus, the High King, the King of Kings, has paid a ransom sufficient to release us all.

---

10. Webster, *In Debt to Christ*, 83–84.

The picture of Jesus' death as the payment of a ransom invites us to realize is that we are captives, that we are hostages to the powers of evil, sin, and death. In Colossians 1, Jesus is seen as God's agent through whom God the Father has delivered us from one realm, the domain of darkness, and transferred us to another, his own kingdom (Col 1:13). We are like Henry "Box" Brown, who was transported to freedom from Virginia to Pennsylvania in a wooden crate through the postal system. We were in a slave state, but Jesus' actions have moved us into a free state. We needed Jesus to pay the price because, as captives, we cannot release ourselves. The ransom metaphor highlights the total impossibility of us doing anything to achieve our own salvation.

The gratuity of our rescue

Our rescue from captivity is free in two senses. As we have seen, it is free in the sense that we can contribute nothing to our own rescue. Even our ability to admit that we are in captivity depends on the Holy Spirit.

It is also free in the sense that Jesus could have chosen not to rescue us at all. Like the Somali taxi driver who raised the money which freed the Chandlers or the friends of Sahil Saeed's family who sold their jewelry to help pay his ransom, Jesus was under no obligation to intervene to rescue us. Sometimes we think of God as someone sat on a cloud somewhere, in supreme indifference to the plight of humanity. The God of the Bible, the living God, is not like that at all. Although there are points at which God could have destroyed humanity and started again (Gen 6:6–7) or could have rejected Israel and chosen another holy people (Exod 32:10), God has chosen to rescue and to restore. God did so because God loves us and because, as a result of his love for us, he has promised to redeem us (Deut 7:8). This God, our God, is our loving heavenly father, who sent his one and only Son on a rescue mission which cost him his life but which broke open the gates of hell and released the stranglehold of the powers of evil, sin, selfishness, and death.

Problems with the ransom metaphor

To whom is the ransom paid?

The major difficulty with the ransom metaphor comes when the idea of the ransom is taken too literally. When this becomes the focus for our exploration, a number of difficult questions seem to arise. To whom is the ransom paid? If the answer is the devil, then this seems to suggest that the devil somehow has acquired rights over sinful human beings and must be paid off. If the answer is God, then this raises questions about what God is really like. We will look at each of these suggestions in turn.

If the devil is paid the ransom, does this mean that the devil has rights over sinful human beings?

Some early and medieval theologians thought that, by sinning, Adam and Eve handed themselves over to Satan (this theory can be found in the twelfth-century *Liber Pancrisis*). Because Adam and Eve had done so voluntarily, he gained rights over them as their lord. As a consequence, all human beings became rightfully subject to Satan. When God became man in Christ, Satan sought to extend his lordship over Christ; but because the attempt failed because Christ was sinless and resisted Satan's temptation. By overreaching himself in wrongfully seeking to claim lordship over Christ, Satan forfeited his rights over the rest of humanity. Christ, as the wronged party, acquired the jurisdiction Satan had forfeited by his own unlawful act.

Tooting Bec, in South London, which I lived near for many years, was land belonging to the abbey of Bec in Normandy (from where it gets its name). Anselm (1033–1109), who became archbishop of Canterbury, was abbot of the abbey of Bec. He did not find this interpretation of the ransom theory convincing. He was adamant that the devil, who was a traitor against God, a liar, and a thief, did not have just dominion over human beings.

Anselm developed his own theory, the satisfaction theory of the atonement, as a reaction against this idea. For Anselm, only God has rights, the right to be obeyed by God's creatures. The devil's jurisdiction over human beings is only ever a matter of fact and never a matter of right. Like the White Witch in *The Lion, the Witch and the Wardrobe*, the devil is a usurper. The might of evil does not make evil's hold over human beings right. Just like the kidnappers of the Chandlers and of Sahil Saeed, the devil has power over human beings which he has no right to.

Anselm's view seems to be supported by Acts 10:38, which is translated in the Christian Standard Bible (CSB) as, "God anointed Jesus of Nazareth with the Holy Spirit and with power, and ... He went about doing good and curing all who were under the tyranny of the Devil."

T. F. Torrance agrees with Anselm that "the whole notion of ransom paid to an evil power is impossible on the biblical view ... [In Romans 3:21–25 and the whole of the apostle Paul's thinking] evil is revealed as having no right over man, and to have usurped the right of the law of God and through that right to have robbed God of his inheritance in his people and of his people of their inheritance in God."[11]

If the devil isn't paid the ransom, then how is humanity freed?

Another disturbing consequence of conceding that Satan had rights over human beings was what it implied about how Satan had lost those rights. Satan's rights were the result of human beings having sinned. Because Jesus had never sinned, Satan had no rights over Jesus. Satan's attempt to claim rights over Jesus resulted in him forfeiting his rights over human beings. Attempting to explain how Satan had lost his rights, some ancient theologians (most notably Gregory of Nyssa) suggested that God had hidden

---

11. Torrance, *Atonement*, 30.

Jesus' deity from Satan so that Satan, thinking he was dealing with a mere human, had been tricked by God into overplaying his hand.

René Girard is surely correct that the release of humanity from the power of evil "does not include the least bit of . . . dishonesty on God's part. It is not really a ruse or a trick; it is rather the inability of the prince of this world to understand the divine love." It is Satan himself who "transforms his own mechanism into a trap, and he falls into it headlong."[12]

Satan, in his pride, cannot imagine loving anything other than himself. As a result, Satan is completely blind to the possibility that Jesus might sacrifice himself in order to ransom others. J. K. Rowling's series of novels about Harry Potter and his friends illustrate how an evil being could be blind to the motivations and power of goodness. Voldemort, the most powerful wizard who has ever lived, loves no one other than himself and has no friends, only servants. In *Harry Potter and the Goblet of Fire*, we learn that Voldemort murdered his own father and grandparents. In the course of the seven books, Harry does not defeat Voldemort at his own game; instead it is the love, friendship, and cooperation of Harry with his close friends Hermione and Ron but also the contribution of many others including Hagrid and Neville Longbottom which see Harry through the various challenges he faces.

Look a little deeper, however, and Voldemort is defeated by something he cannot comprehend: the power of self-sacrifice. Harry's mother, Lily, sacrifices her only life to save that of her son in the cottage in Godric's Hollow. Sirius Black steps between Harry and Bellatrix in the battle at the Department of Mysteries, and Professor Dumbledore drinks the poison of a horcrux so that Voldemort might be destroyed.

It is not much of an imaginative leap to read the Harry Potter books as a metaphor of Harry and his friends working out their own salvation in friendship (*koinonia*) and in grateful response to the graceful love to which they contributed nothing.

---

12. Girard, *I See Satan*, 152.

Ransomed, Redeemed, and Forgiven

If the ransom is paid to God, what sort of God are we dealing with?

An alternative way of making sure that the devil has no rights over human beings is to suggest that the ransom was not paid to the devil at all but rather to God the Father. The picture here is of God the Father as the one whom human beings have offended by their actions. God the Father is angry and hurt by human beings' actions. He must be compensated for the wrong which we have done to him. Only then will he look kindly on us once again. Jesus, God the Son, through his death, pays the ransom which God the Father demands and as a result pacifies the Father's wrath.

The problem with this approach to the metaphor is the picture of God it suggests. Christians do not believe in three gods but in one God. This picture risks suggesting that God the Father hates human beings while at the same time God the Son who loves human beings is working to turn the Father's hatred into love. This implies that the triune God has a split personality, with one Person of the Trinity hating humanity whilst another Person of the Trinity loves humanity. Such a view of God is not what the Bible teaches. John 3:16 tells us that God (the Father) so loved the world that he gave his one and only Son. The Father and the Son both love humanity and agreed together that the Son should ransom us from sin, evil, and death.

We don't need to work out to whom the ransom is paid

Gregory of Nazianus (c. 325–89 AD) rejected the idea that on the cross God paid the devil. He recognized that at this point the ransom metaphor has reached its limit: "I enquire to whom was the blood of God poured out? If to the evil one—alas! that the blood of Christ should be offered to the wicked one! But if you say 'To God'—how shall that be, when it is to another (than God) that we were enslaved?"[13]

---

13. Gregory of Nazianus, "Dogmatic Poems," I.viii.65–69.

We were under the reign of the devil, sold to sin, after we had gained corruption on account of our sinful desire. If the price of our ransom is paid to him who has us in his power, I ask myself: Why is such a price to be paid? If it is given to the devil, it is outrageous! The brigand receives the price of redemption. Not only does he receive it from God, he receives God Himself. For his violence he demands such a disproportionate ransom that it would be more just for him to set us free without ransom.

But if the price is paid to the Father, why should that be done? It is not the Father who has held us as His captives. Moreover, why should the blood of His only Son be acceptable to the Father, who did not wish to accept Isaac, when Abraham offered Him his son as a burnt offering, but replaced the human sacrifice with the sacrifice of a ram? Is it not evident that the Father accepts the sacrifice not because He demanded it or had any need for it but by His dispensation? It was necessary that man should be sanctified by the humanity of God; it was necessary that He Himself should free us, triumphing over the tyrant by His own strength . . . Let the rest of the mystery be venerated silently.[14]

Gregory of Nazianus highlights the limits of the ransom metaphor, the point at which it ceases to be helpful. The ransom metaphor tells us that we are captives to the powers of evil, and that God the Father, God the Son and God the Holy Spirit pulled off the most amazing rescue mission, though we will never be able to get to the bottom of how they did it.

Conclusion

The image of Jesus' death as a ransom shows us that we are captives to the powers of evil, that there is nothing we can do to save ourselves, but that in this desperate situation, our true King took part in a hostage exchange, which effected our release by some means we cannot fully comprehend.

---

14. Gregory of Nazianus, *Oration 45*, 22.

Ransomed, Redeemed, and Forgiven

The ransom metaphor is very closely linked to the redemption metaphor, but whereas the ransom metaphor emphasizes the gravity of the situation we need rescuing from, redemption directs our attention to the identity of our rescuer and to the price he was willing to pay in order to release us from our captivity. It is those ideas we will explore in the next chapter.

Redemption and the Cost of Salvation

"Redemption . . . is the very center of the Christian faith"
P. T. FORSYTH, *THE WORK OF CHRIST*

What does it mean to redeem something?

Redemption from the pawnbroker

FOR MANY YEARS I lived in Tooting in South London. The neighborhood had a number of pawnbrokers, easily identifiable by the three golden balls hanging outside their shops (the three golden balls were originally the symbol of the Medicis). Pawnbrokers have, for centuries, offered emergency loans to the poor.

The pawnbroker lends money against security. The borrower has to hand over something to get the pawnbroker to give her the money. Watches, jewelry, coats, blankets, tools may all be accepted by the pawnbroker as security. What the pawnbroker is looking for is something that is easy to store and easy to sell. The object is held by the pawnbroker in pledge, acting as a back-up to the borrower's promise to repay the loan.

All the borrower has to do in order to get back the objects they have pawned is to repay the loan (plus interest, of course) by the date specified by the pawnbroker. If the borrower cannot do so, the pawnbroker doesn't have to worry about finding the borrower, suing the borrower, or forcing the borrower to repay the loan. The pawnbroker simply sells the pawned item in order to pay off the loan.

Because this is how pawnbroking works, the pawnbroker will never give you the full value for the objects you pawn. By offering up an object as a pledge, the borrower has put that object in jeopardy, risking something valuable for the sake of cash in the here and now. To get the object back, the loan has to be repaid on time. If the loan is repaid, the pawned object is redeemed; it is released by the pawnbroker and returned to its rightful owner. If the loan is not repaid; it is forfeited to the pawnbroker. The borrower loses their rights of ownership and the pawnbroker becomes the legal owner of the object.

Because of that risk, resort to a pawnbroker can be a sign of desperation. Bon Jovi's 1980s rock anthem, *Living on a Prayer*, tells us that Tommy is a dockworker whose union are on strike. Without his paycheck coming in, Tommy has had to pawn (hock) his most treasured possession, his six-string guitar.

Emma Abbott

The first entry in *Brainard's Biographies of American Musicians* tells the story of the nineteenth-century singer Emma Abbott. On a concert tour, Emma played three concerts in Monroe, Michigan. Bad weather meant the audiences were poor and she wasn't able to pay her hotel bill. The landlord seized her guitar as security. Fortunately, Emma got some work singing with an opera company and was able to redeem her guitar.

On her next tour, at Plymouth, Indiana, she was so hard up that she had to pawn not only her guitar but also her concert dress. Thanks to the kindness of a clerk from a music shop who offered to accompany her on the piano, she was able to earn $18 from singing in Fort Wayne and so to redeem both her dress and her guitar.

Emma's experience shows vividly how disastrous it can be if something is not redeemed, and how we may need outside help in order to be able to do so.

Debt-slavery

What do you do if you don't have anything you can offer up as security? This was a real problem in biblical times. Sometimes the poor were driven to desperate measures: offering as security the coat they slept under at night or, like Emma Abbott, the tools they needed to earn their living. The law of Moses contains specific warnings against creditors holding on to such pledges overnight (Exod 22:26; Deut 24:12).

Things could get even worse. Once a borrower had pawned everything they owned, the only things left to offer as pledges were their children or themselves. The law of Moses contains passages such as Leviticus 25 which make uncomfortable reading but which reflect the economic reality of the times: someone driven by famine or other disaster could find themselves having to sell themselves into slavery in order to avoid starvation.

This type of debt-slavery (also known as "debt bondage," "bonded slavery," or "modern slavery") persists across the world today, blighting the lives of millions of men, women, and children. Time and again, throughout time and across the globe, the poor get into debt when tragedy or disaster happens. When crops fail, the poor may have to borrow money to feed their children. When injury or illness strikes, money may be needed to pay a doctor. Desperate, and with no access to anything that we would recognize as a bank, they borrow money from the local moneylender. The problem is the terms on which the money is lent: the loan must be paid back in full in a single sum—installments are not acceptable. In order to guarantee the payment of "interest" until such time as the family can afford to repay the full sum, one or more family members must work as a bonded laborer. Deprived of that person's labor, the family's finances become even more stretched, and the loan can never be paid off.

The realities of debt-slavery today are brutal. Debt-slaves are forced to work long hours, often seven days a week, for an employer who is also their creditor. Unable to leave to find work elsewhere, they are paid pitifully low wages which leave them with little or no chance of ever paying off the interest on their debt. Physical and sexual abuse are commonplace. In some cases, slaves are locked in small cages or rooms. Collective punishment, intimidation, and violence are used to break their will and to keep them in line. Often, not only the original borrower but also their children become slaves to the creditor, beaten and abused, denied their basic rights and any dignity.

In 2016, the International Labour Organization estimated that there may be more than forty million people held in bonded slavery today.[1] That is a very conservative figure. According to Human Rights Watch, in India alone there may be as many as 15 million *children* in bonded slavery.[2]

Though illegal in most countries round the world, in many places law enforcement agencies turn a blind eye to the practice (especially when bribed or threatened by the moneylenders). International Justice Mission (IJM) is a Christian organization which investigates such cases and applies pressure in the right places to release the captives. Here are some of the stories they report:

Chinnanan's story

At age fifty-five, Chinnanan became a debt-slave in a South Asian country. Twenty years later, he and forty-one other members of his family were still working as slaves in a quarry to pay off that debt. When Moses started standing up for the Israelites in Egypt, their working conditions were made worse. In the same way, when the slave owners learned of IJM's investigation, they started withholding daily supplies of food and water from Chinnanan's family

---

1. Kardol, "Five Interesting Facts."
2. Neff, "Meanwhile: For 15 Million in India, a Childhood of Slavery."

and the other workers in their quarry. The families were forced to sell what few possessions they had left in order to afford only one meal a day to survive. Once IJM had gathered enough evidence, local authorities were forced to act, leading to the release of a total of 117 people held in bondage and the arrests of six of the owners who had enslaved them.

Narakalappa's story

In another rescue carried out in June 2003, IJM rescued sixteen slaves, including Narakalappa, a seventy-year-old man who had been born into slavery. He, his children, and his grandchildren all worked as slaves on an agricultural plantation, trapped by debts inherited from previous generations.

Sadeepan's story

In 2008, International Justice Mission heard of another rock quarry where slaves were being held. The slaves had been trafficked to the quarry, reducing their chances of escape because they did not speak the local language. Controlled by beatings, threats, and verbal abuse, the slaves were forced to break boulders using hand mallets and spent their days carrying heavy rocks. So terrible were the conditions that the laborers found ways to make contact with the outside world, despite the fact that leaving the facility without permission could result in a severe beating or other violent attack from the owners. In early August 2008, two slaves managed to escape from the facility. The owners reacted by holding two other slaves, a young father named Sadeepan and another man, responsible. The owners beat Sadeepan, bound him with a yellow rope, and locked him up in a small room at night. IJM collated evidence of the slavery, and together with forty police officers entered the quarry on September 11, 2008, to release the slaves.

The exodus is God redeeming Israel from slavery

The exodus story is literally a story about redemption from slavery. Egypt is described as the land of slavery in Exodus (2:23; 13:3, 14; 20:2), Deuteronomy (5:6; 6:12; 7:8; 8:14; 13:5; 15:15; 24:18), Joshua (24:17), and Judges (6:8). The Israelites were bought out of their slavery by God (YHWH).

The Old Testament describes the rescue of the Israelites from Egypt using three different Hebrew words. The words *padah*, *kipper*, and *go'el* each highlight a different aspect of the way in which Jesus has ransomed and redeemed us. T. F. Torrance suggests that *padah* highlights how Christ is the victor over evil, sin, and death; that *kipper* pictures Christ as the sacrificial lamb, as the victim whose shed blood is the price of our redemption; and that Christ as our *go'el* is our surety, the one who "stands in for us, so that it is *in him* that we have redemption."[3] The three words therefore place the emphasis on what was achieved *(padah)*, on the cost of the achievement *(kipper)* and on who achieved it *(go'el)*. We've already looked at the first of those in the previous chapter; in this chapter we will explore on the remaining two.

The Torah describes two dimensions of God's rescue of the Israelites from slavery. One dimension is God's rescue of the Israelites from the dark powers of the Egyptian gods. The Egyptians worshipped a whole pantheon of gods, some, like Osiris, Isis, and Horus, associated with the river Nile, others with health and livestock, leading up to the chief god, Amun, the sun-god. In the plagues, YHWH, the Lord God of Israel defeats these Egyptian gods one by one. The Nile is polluted (Exod 7:14–24), all the way through until the ninth plague, when Amun is exposed and darkness covers the land (Exod 10:21–29).

The final plague brings into focus the other dimension of God's rescue. Exodus 11 and 12 describe the Passover. Exodus 12:12 explains: "I will pass through Egypt and strike down every firstborn—both men and animals—and I will bring judgment on all the gods of Egypt. I am the Lord. The blood will be a sign for

---

3. Torrance, *Atonement*, 175.

you on the houses where you are; and when I see the blood, I will pass over you."

There was only one way to avoid the plague: be inside a house which has lamb's blood smeared on the door frame. The killing of a lamb was a heavy price for a family to pay. Remember that the Israelites were slaves in Egypt. In England, for many centuries, sheep were so valuable a piece of property that anyone who stole one would be hanged. Hence the saying, "Might as well be hanged for a sheep as a lamb." The slaughter of a lamb and the daubing of its blood on the door frame was not some sort of magical act; it was the demonstration of faith, that those inside the house trusted in the power of YHWH to protect them from death and that they were willing to put everything on the line because of that trust.

There is, however, no escaping the uncomfortable fact that the price of Israel's redemption was paid not only by the blood of the lambs killed to provide the first Passover meal but also by the firstborn sons of the Egyptians, who died because of the intransigence of Pharaoh and in recompense for his genocidal policies (see Exod 1). The price of Israel's redemption was both that of an innocent lamb and of a firstborn son dying on behalf of the guilty.

We belong to God because God has bought us
(Lev 25:42, 55)

When someone is saved from death by someone, they may say in response, "I owe you my life." On November 29, 2019, Rhiannon Owen was a student nurse using a cash machine near London Bridge when a man wielding knives began attacking people at random. Seeing that Ms. Owen was unaware of what was happening, a taxi driver pulled over and shouted at her "Please run, you've got to run now." Interviewed after the incident, Ms. Owen said, "I don't know who you are, but I owe you my life."

The sixteenth-century Heidelberg Catechism shows us why we owe our lives to Jesus in its very first question. It asks, "What is my only comfort in life and in death?"[4] The answer is: *"That I am not my own*, but belong—body and soul, in life and in death—to my faithful Savior, Jesus Christ. He has fully paid for all my sins with his precious blood, and has set me free from the tyranny of the devil. He also watches over me in such a way that not a hair can fall from my head without the will of my Father in heaven; in fact, all things must work together for my salvation. *Because I belong to him*, Christ, by his Holy Spirit, assures me of eternal life and makes me wholeheartedly willing and ready from now on to live for him."

Isaiah 43:1 says, "But now, this is what the LORD says—he who created you, O Jacob, he who formed you, O Israel: 'Fear not, for I have redeemed you; I have summoned you by name; you are mine.'" This one verse brings together all the reasons why we belong to God: we belong to God because God created us, we belong to God because God has redeemed us; we belong to God because God has called us.

In the ancient world, a freed slave who did not own any land and who did not have any special skills was perhaps more vulnerable to destitution and starvation than a slave. Slaves, especially those working on a farm or in a household, could at least expect their owners to feel that it was in their best interests to keep their slaves fed. Day laborers, though free, were vulnerable to starvation if there was no work to be found.

In Roman society, this situation was addressed through the idea of patronage. A freed slave would remain associated with their patron. The freed slave was still expected to show gratitude and loyalty to their former master who was, in turn, expected to provide work and protection to the ex-slave. As we shall see in our last chapter, the extraordinary good news is that God the Father goes beyond acting as our patron; he actually adopts those he has freed as his children.

---

2. "Heidelberg Catechism."

The impact of the exodus on Israel's law

In the exodus story, the word *goël* emphasizes the fact that God rescued the Israelites because they belonged to him (Exod 6:6; 15:13). The woman forced to pawn her wedding ring will do whatever she can to raise the money to redeem it not because of the value of the metal but because of what it means to her. Because God had redeemed the Israelites from slavery in Egypt, they belonged to God, and God was the ultimate owner of the land which God gave to them. As a consequence, Israel's laws included rules allowing property and people to be redeemed (Lev 25).

The Passover lamb

As we noted in our opening chapter, the ideas of ransom and redemption are very closely linked in both the Old and New Testaments. The images bleed into one another. In the Old Testament, the verb *padah* (which we have translated as "to ransom") is found together with the noun *kopher* ("redemption"), formed from the verb *kipper*, in Psalm 49 and Job 33. T. F. Torrance explains that in those passages, the "noun *kopher* is used to describe the *price* of the redemption described by the verb *padah*. That brings these aspects into the closest relation . . . If the term *padah* has to do with redemption from the power of sin, the term *kipper* has to do rather with redemption as the actual wiping out of sin and guilt."[5]

We looked at Psalm 49 in our last chapter. T. F. Torrance translates Psalm 49:7–9 as, "Truly no man can ransom (*padah*) himself (or his brother), or give to God the price (*kopher*) of his life, for the ransom (*pidyon*) of his life is costly, and can never suffice that he should continue to live on for ever and never see the Pit . . . But God will ransom (*padah*) my soul from the power of Sheol, for he will receive me."[6]

In John's Gospel, John the Baptist describes Jesus as the Lamb of God who takes away the sin of the world (John 1:29). Jesus fulfills

---

5. Torrance, *Atonement*, 33, italics original.
6. Torrance, *Atonement*, 35.

the functions of various different lambs and goats described in the Old Testament. Jesus is the Passover lamb whose blood redeems God's people (1 Cor 5:7); Jesus is also the goat sacrificed as a sin offering on the Day of Atonement (Yom Kippur).

Sacrifice and compounding

A moment's reflection will confirm that we all owe our whole lives to God. God is the one who created the universe, the planet on which life is possible, and who is the ultimate cause of the processes through which we were conceived, born, and are sustained. How can we ever repay God? The conundrum here is, as Isaac Watts expressed it, *were the whole nature of mine, that is an offering far too small?*[7]

Many civilizations have faced this question. Since they all ruled out self-immolation (or the ones which did not last only a moment in history), the general answer was some sort of sacrifice *pars pro toto*, some offering to God in thankfulness for one's life. All too often, the sacrifice chosen was one of one's own children. The story of Abraham's near-sacrifice of Isaac in Genesis 22 ruled out child sacrifice as an option for the Jews. Instead, the Old Testament cult centered around animal sacrifice.

The logic of sacrifice is the logic of what lawyers sometimes call "compounding." If I owe someone £1,000 and I cannot pay it, I may meet with my creditor and offer him £600 now, in settlement of the debt. If my creditor accepts the offer, then I have compounded with him. I have been released from the full extent of my obligation by offering a lesser sum.

A farmer who, thanks to the goodness of God in sending the sun and the rain, owes the whole of his crop to God could compound that obligation by offering God the firstfruits of his crop (Exod 23:19; Lev 23:10; Deut 18:4).

Because God had redeemed God's people from slavery in Egypt, they all belonged to God. The reminder to God's people

---

7 Watts, "When I Survey."

Redemption and the Cost of Salvation

of that reality was the setting aside of every firstborn male (Exod 13:1-2). To be set apart is to be holy. The Israelites are called, in the Hebrew Scriptures, to recognize that they have been redeemed by God by acknowledging that some things are to be set apart for God.

Exodus 13:14-16 explains:

> In days to come, when your son asks you, "What does this mean?" say to him, "With a mighty hand the Lord brought us out of Egypt, out of the land of slavery. When Pharaoh stubbornly refused to let us go, the Lord killed the firstborn of both people and animals in Egypt. This is why I sacrifice to the Lord the first male offspring of every womb and redeem each of my firstborn sons." And it will be like a sign on your hand and a symbol on your forehead that the Lord brought us out of Egypt with his mighty hand.

The rescue of the Israelites from Egypt was reflected in Israel's law stipulating that firstborn animals and sons belong to God. However, God will accept substitutes. Numbers 3:11-13 specifies that the Levites belong to God in place of the first male offspring of every Israelite woman:

> The Lord also said to Moses, "I have taken the Levites from among the Israelites in place of the first male offspring of every Israelite woman. The Levites are mine, for all the firstborn are mine. When I struck down all the firstborn in Egypt, I set apart for myself every firstborn in Israel, whether human or animal. They are to be mine. I am the Lord."

The chapter continues with a headcount of the Levites which reveals that there were 273 more firstborn Israelites than Levites. Those 273 extra firstborns had to be redeemed at a cost of five shekels each (Num 3:44-51), which was collected and set apart for use by the priests. The same tariff of five shekels was the redemption price for each firstborn son and each firstborn male of unclean animals (Num 18:16). The people of Israel as a whole owed everything to God, but God accepted the service of the Levites in lieu.

The idea of compounding applies when someone makes a monetary payment instead of experiencing the punishment that would otherwise be due to them. In the Germanic Laws that applied in the Dark Ages in Germany, France, and Anglo-Saxon England, a killer could avoid the death penalty by paying a *weregild*, a man-price. The payment of the *weregild* redeemed the debt of punishment created by the death.

The Hebrew Scriptures prohibit compounding for certain offences (Lev 27:29, Num 35:31–32) but there are some passages which refer to it expressly. Exodus 21:28–32 discuss a number of tragic cases which can happen on a farm. There are four scenarios: in one a man or a woman is killed in an unexpected attack by a bull, in the other three scenarios someone, either a freeman or woman, a child, or a slave is killed by a bull which was in the habit of goring and which had not been securely penned up by its owner. In each of the four scenarios discussed, someone has been killed by a bull. In each instance, the bull has to be stoned to death. Where what happened was a freak accident, matters end there. But in the other three scenarios, the bull was in the habit of goring; the owner had been warned about it but had failed to keep the bull penned up (verse 29). Because of the owner's carelessness, the owner as well as the bull should be put to death. But, the family of the victim had the option of asking the owner for blood money instead. Verse 30 says, "*If* payment is demanded of him, he may redeem his life by repaying whatever is demanded." In this instance, the Old Testament expressly allowed the payment of a *weregild* if one was demanded by the victim's family.

The Year of Jubilee

A striking feature of Israel's laws is the Year of Jubilee (Lev 25:8–55). Every fifty years, debts were to be cancelled and land was to be returned to the family which originally owned it. The provisions for resetting the economy seem so dramatic that for a long time it was questioned whether such a Jubilee could ever have been applied in practice.

However, Assyriologists have discovered that debt amnesties were in fact a common feature of ancient Near East politics, dating as far back as 2400 BC, when Enmetena, ruler of the city of Lagash in Sumer, cancelled agrarian debts. The practice became commonplace among Sumerian kings and was taken up by Babylonian kings in the dynasty of Hammurabi. Michael Hudson explores the evidence in. . . . *And Forgive Them Their Debts: Lending, Foreclosure, and Redemption from Bronze Age Finance to the Jubilee Year* (2018).

The idea of debt jubilees still resonates today. Jubilee was a compelling slogan for the Jubilee 2000 debt campaign, which led to the cancellation of more than one hundred billion dollars of debt owed by thirty-five of the world's poorest countries at the turn of the millennium.

In the United States of America, everyone wants to know what legislation the president will want to introduce during his first one hundred days. In the ancient Near East, very often a new ruler would announce a debt amnesty when they took power. Such a measure would ensure their popularity with the people, would demonstrate their confidence in their country's economic future, and would be a sign of their magnanimity and determination to defend the poor.

In Israel, God was Israel's king. The Year of Jubilee was God's standing legislation, meant to provide a predictable resetting of the Israelite economy to which everyone could look forward.

The first purpose of the Jubilee was to prevent debt-slavery being passed down the generations. In ancient Israel, economic security depended on having access to land to farm and not having unpayable debts to service. In the Year of Jubilee, a family was supposed to get back its ancestral lands and get rid of its ongoing debt. The next generation was given a fresh start, the opportunity to make a go of it without being crushed by the effects of the disasters or disadvantages inherited from the past. The Year of Jubilee represented the ongoing commitment of Israel's God that the Israelites never, ever would be slaves. God who had redeemed Israel as a nation from slavery was, through the institution of the Jubilee, still actively committed to redeeming Israelite families from slavery.

The Jubilee year looks forward to the Day of Christ, "for it is his coming which achieves for us the cancellation of all debt and the restoration to us of the rights we had forfeited as God's creatures and as members of God's family and household."[8]

Jesus' Nazareth Manifesto in Luke 4 is his declaration of the key objectives of his reign. The Nazareth Manifesto was the equivalent of Jesus announcing the program for the first one hundred days of his presidency. Jesus declares that he will bring about the Year of the Lord's Favor, that he will bring good news to the poor, release those imprisoned for debt, and set free those in slavery (Luke 4:18–19). He announces that there will be a Jubilee in which he will cancel all debts. In the same way that ancient Assyrian rulers had announced a Jubilee as their first political act, so Jesus was going public with his mission to end oppression, slavery, and captivity.

The kinsman-redeemer

The word "redemption" literally means to buy back or to win back something which has been lost. The *goël* is the kinsman-redeemer, the one with responsibility to bail a relative out of bankruptcy, slavery, or forfeiture of their lands, possessions, and other rights.

A key role of the *goël* was to hunt down the murderer of a kinsman (Num 35:19). One of my favorite countries in the world is Albania. In the mountains of Albania, villagers once lived according to customary law. This law prescribed if that if someone was killed, their nearest male relative was under a duty to avenge their death. In *Broken April*, the brilliant Albanian novelist Ismail Kadaré explores the story of Gjorg. Gjorg has to avenge his brother's death, but by doing so becomes liable to being killed by his brother's killer's avenger. The kinsman has to be prepared to

---

8. Torrance, *Atonement*, 50.

sacrifice his own life to avenge his family's honor. And so the cycle of vendetta continues. This custom was widespread well into the twentieth century, and there are still examples of these vendettas occurring today. Jesus is our *go'el*, our avenger, but one who breaks the cycle of death by destroying the man-slayer death itself.

Western societies are so individualist in their mindset that the idea of a kinsman-redeemer can seem very strange. But we find it in an important sub-plot in series 1 of the Netflix hit *Bridgerton*. Miss Marina Thompson is a cousin of the Featherington family. When she arrives with them for the summer season, she is already pregnant by Sir George Crane. He is a soldier who has gone off to war, unaware that he has fathered a child and without having married Miss Thompson. Miss Thompson writes to him, but her letters go unanswered. Miss Thompson endures a topsy-turvy season during which her pregnancy is concealed and she is hawked out to rich old men only interested in acquiring a trophy wife while she waits in desperation for news from her lover.

One day, Sir George's younger brother, Sir Phillip Crane, comes to call. He brings news that Sir George is dead and comes to return Miss Thompson's letters to her. He knows that she is pregnant with his brother's child. He proposes marriage to her. In so doing, Sir Philip is acting as a kinsman-redeemer. What he is doing is very similar to the custom of levirate marriage, in which if one brother died without having fathered any children, his surviving brother was under an obligation (which he could refuse) to marry the widow (Deut 25:5–9).

The custom of levirate marriage is key to the plot of the book of Ruth. Ruth, a Moabite, married her husband after his family had moved to Moab to escape a famine (Ruth 1). Ruth's husband had died, leaving her widowed and childless. Despite this, she follows her mother-in-law Naomi back to Bethlehem, where the two women scratch a living scavenging grain left over after the harvest. Ruth's commitment to her mother-in-law in this desperate existence earns the respect of Boaz, the farmer in whose fields she has been gathering grain and a relative of her husband's family (Ruth 3:10–13). Boaz offers to marry Ruth, but the love-match can only be concluded once the nearest kinsman-redeemer has refused to step in (Ruth 4:5). Boaz's marriage to Ruth leads to her husband's family's land being retained and to Ruth becoming a mother, and an ancestor of King David and of Jesus Christ. Boaz, by taking on the responsibility of the kinsman-redeemer, gives Ruth love, security, and hope within the community of God's people.

The idea of the kinsman-redeemer formalizes what is a natural human response. When the father of a teenage son discovers that the son has been arrested for joy-riding, what does the father do? He goes down to the police station and he pays the bail to get his son out of the cell. When someone who belongs with us is in trouble, we want to help them out, if necessary paying off what they owe.

The Old Testament pictures God as Israel's kinsman-redeemer. Leviticus 25 contains a series of detailed provisions by which property and persons who have sold themselves into debt-slavery can be redeemed. Verse 48 describes the plight of the impoverished Israelite who has sold himself into slavery to a foreigner. He should be rescued by his brother, or if not by his brother, by his uncle, or if not by his uncle, by his uncle's son, or if not by his uncle's son, by any one of his blood relatives from his family. But what if there is no family member who is able or willing to redeem him? YHWH's answer, in verses 54–55, is: "'Even if someone is not redeemed in any of these ways, they and their children are to be released in the Year of Jubilee, for the Israelites belong to me as servants. They are my servants, whom I brought out of Egypt. I am the Lord your God."

God is Israel's true owner, the one to whom we truly belong (Ps 34:22); God is Israel's king rescuing his people (Isa 44:6); God is Israel's father who will pay off the debts of his profligate son (Isa 63:16); God is Israel's faithful husband who will rescue his unfaithful wife (Isa 54:5). Isaiah 63:16 says, "You, O Lord, are our Father, our Redeemer [*go'el*] from old is your name." Psalm 74:2 calls on God to "Remember the people you purchased of old, the tribe of your inheritance, whom you redeemed [*gaal*]—Mount Zion, where you dwelt."

The exile as a return to slavery

The loss of political independence and exile which Israel experienced when Judah was conquered by Babylon (and which N. T. Wright argues Israel was still experiencing at the time of Jesus)[9] was likened in Isaiah 50 to debt-slavery. In Isaiah 50:1, God asks, rhetorically: "Which of my creditors is it to whom I have sold you?"

If you were my debt-slave, I could sell you to one of my own creditors to pay off my debt to them. Lawyers refer to debts which can be sold by one person to another as negotiable, and the documents which record such debts as negotiable instruments. The notion is preposterous when applied to God. God, who created heaven and earth out of nothing, has no creditors. God therefore answers God's own question in the negative: "No, because of your sins you were sold."

Isaiah 52 compares the experience of the Jews in exile in Babylon with that of their experience in Egypt. In both cases, "my people have been taken away for nothing" (verse 5). In both cases, they are mocked and oppressed. In both cases, they will be redeemed without money (verse 3). As we saw in the last chapter, Israel's captors are not lawful owners with whom God will enter into a business transaction to secure the release of God's people; they are violators and abusers who are not entitled to the rights they claim.

The Old Testament anticipating redemption from sin and death

The exodus brings together the terrors of physical slavery and of death. The prophets warned Israel against the worship of idols (a return to the worship of gods like the Egyptian gods) and against social injustice (a return to slavery like that experienced in Egypt). Both lead only to captivity. But the prophets also increasingly affirmed the power of YHWH to rescue God's people from sin and death. For example, Isaiah 44:22 says, "I have swept away your

---

9. Wright, *The Climax of the Covenant*, 141.

offenses like a cloud, your sins like the morning mist. Return to me, for I have redeemed you." Hosea 13:14 promises, "I will ransom them from the power of the grave; I will redeem them from death."

The Psalmists realize that we need redemption not just from slavery but also from our other enemies (Ps 69:18; 119:134), from our troubles (Ps 25:22), from sin (Ps 130:7-8), and from death (Ps 49:15; 103:4). Psalm 130 affirms the fullness of the redemption God brings. It is full redemption, redemption from all our sins (verses 7b-8). There is no compromise with sin, death, or the devil. The full price is paid. God's redemption of God's people flows out of God's unfailing love (Ps 44:26) and brings freedom from condemnation.

Job realizes that God is eternal and that one day he will see God face to face (Job 19:25-27). The Psalmist is also able to proclaim that "God will redeem my life from the grave; he will surely take me to himself." (Ps 49:15). Gary Anderson's book *Sin: A History* explains why it was natural for the prophets to apply the metaphor of redemption to death. In earlier parts of the Old Testament, the word-picture most commonly used to describe sin was that of a burden. Sin was seen as something weighing down or oppressing people. In later times, it became more usual to think about sin as being a type of debt. Death was therefore the price you pay if you are unable to repay your debt of sin.

Anderson explains that in Aramaic, the language which Jesus and his disciples spoke, the word *hôbâ* was the word not only for a debt owed to a lender but was also the word typically used to describe sin.[10] *Hôbâ* was translated into Greek as *opheiléma*. When Matthew writes in Matthew 6:12 that in the Lord's Prayer we should pray "forgive us our *opheiléma*," he is remembering vividly hearing Jesus teach that we should ask God to forgive our *hôbâ*. If sin is debt, and death is the interest incurred as a result, then redemption is the obvious way of talking about what needs to be done in order to free us.

---

10. Anderson, *Sin*, 28-31.

The cross as redemption

Redemption from sin and death

In the letter to the Romans, the apostle Paul offers an explanation of why both Jews and Gentiles alike are enslaved to sin and facing the penalty of death. Failing to thank God for God's goodness to them, Gentiles have become trapped into all sorts of idolatry, injustice, immorality and violence (Rom 1:18–32). But Jews too, despite having the law of Moses to guide them, have been guilty of engaging in exactly the same thoughts, words, and behavior (Rom 2). The law of Moses clarified how we should live lives pleasing to God and warned that the penalty for not doing so is death. The effect of the law of Moses, says Paul, is to make us conscious of sin (Rom 3:20) and to warn us that the wages of sin is death (Rom 6:23).

The redemption Paul writes about in his letter to the Romans follows the pattern of the redemption of the exodus. As Alastair Roberts and Andrew Wilson explain:

> Most emphatically, [the exodus] is there in Romans. We were all enslaved to sin, bound by the law, and under the rule of death. But God redeemed us through Jesus Christ (Rom 3:21–26). We were buried with him in baptism, with our old slave master dead in the waters behind us (6:1–14). We immediately found joy in serving our new master (6:15–23), experiencing both freedom from the law (7:1–25) and new life in the Spirit (8:1–11). For now, we continue living as children and heirs, with God's Spirit among us, rather than slipping back into slavery (8:12–17)—but we look forward to the new Land of Promise, in which not only our bodies but creation itself will be set free from slavery to corruption and liberated into the freedom that God's children were always supposed to inherit (8:18–25). With that future in mind, we wait with patience, secure in the love God has demonstrated to us in Christ (8:26–39).[11]

---

11. Roberts and Wilson, *Echoes of Exodus*, 144.

The cost of our redemption

The ideas of ransom (*lutron*) and redemption (*apolutrosis*) are closely connected in Greek. T. F. Torrance helps us understand their connection: "The term which the New Testament uses for redemption, *apolutrosis*, is derived not from the verb but from the noun *lutron*, which refers not so much to the act as to the cost of redemption. That should warn us that any account of redemption in the New Testament and early church which does not give central significance to the *lutron*, the price of redemption, is hardly likely to do justice to their understanding."[12]

The word-picture of redemption focuses our attention on the cost of our rescue. In our previous chapter, we learned how rescuing the Chandlers and Sahil Saaed cost hundreds of thousands of pounds (or dollars) in each case. Rescuing you and me, rescuing the human race, cost Jesus his life. The cost of overcoming the power of evil, sin, selfishness and death was the death of the Son of God. That's at the heart of the picture of Jesus' death as our redemption. It's the supreme cost which Jesus bore which was the focus of the church's reflections on the cross.

In the letter to the Galatians, Paul describes the penalty of death as the curse of the law. The Greek for marketplace is *agora*, and in Galatians 3:13 the verb used to describe Christ's action is *exagorazó*. Christ went into the slave market and bought us. He has bought us back; He has bought us out of our indebtedness. Galatians 3:13 tells us that "Christ [bought us out] from the curse of the law by becoming a curse for us, for it is written: 'Cursed is everyone who is hung on a tree.'" Paul is quoting there from Deuteronomy 21:23, which says that a man guilty of a capital offence is to be put to death by handing on a tree. The cost of our salvation was Jesus undergoing a death he did not deserve but we did.

Fleming Rutledge is uncompromising on this point: "In the death of Jesus we see God himself suffering the consequences of Sin. That is the 'price.' When Christian teaching falls short of this

---

12. Torrance, *Atonement*, 26.

proclamation, the work of Christ is diminished to the vanishing point."[13]

The message of the cross is that God loved us so much that God was prepared to pay the price of death in order to rescue us, who are the hostages of the powers of evil, sin, and death. In Matthew 20:19, Jesus predicted not only his death but that "On the third day he will be raised to life." The message of Easter Sunday is that the rescue mission was a success, that the power of death has been broken, and that one day we will experience the fullness of freedom from those powers which have held us captive and from whose grip we have not yet entirely escaped. In C. S. Lewis's story *The Lion, the Witch and the Wardrobe*, the Stone Table on which Aslan was killed is broken in two.

The price paid was the blood of Jesus

Growing up in the 1970s, the hymn book we used in church was the *Redemptional Hymnal*. I didn't understand at the time, but its bright scarlet cover was obviously chosen to remind us that the price of our redemption was the blood of Jesus. The twenty-first century hymn by Keith Getty and Stuart Townend, "In Christ Alone My Hope Is Found" (2001), proclaims that "I am his and he is mine, Bought with the precious blood of Christ."

The price of our redemption is the blood of Jesus. This should have been obvious to the early disciples even if Jesus had not spelled it out in terms at the Last Supper: "This is the new covenant in my blood" (Luke 22:20; 1 Cor 11:25). Every Jew knew that the price of their redemption from slavery in Egypt had been the blood of a lamb. But, as we have seen, Jesus was also the firstborn son, dying on behalf of the guilty.

Alastair Roberts and Andrew Wilson draw out the depth of the link between the Passover and the Last Supper:

> It is not just that the Last Supper evokes the Passover in hindsight; it is that the Passover evokes the Last Supper

13. Rutledge, *The Crucifixion*, 287.

> in advance. Jesus' broken body and spilled blood, in some mysterious way, is bound up with the fact that Israel ate matzot and drank wine in the first place. The deliverance from slavery to Pharaoh was always going to be fulfilled in the deliverance from slavery to sin. The Mosaic covenant builds toward the new covenant. Passover culminates in Eucharist.[14]

Revelation 5:9 is one of many verses in the New Testament that are explicit that the price of our redemption was paid in Jesus' blood: "You were slain, and with your blood you purchased for God persons from every tribe and language and people and nation." In 1 Peter 1:18–19, it is emphasized that the price of our salvation was not paid "with perishable things such as silver and gold, but with the precious blood of Christ, like that of a lamb without blemish or spot."

Whatever one makes of some of the conclusions reached by the Synod of Dort, its second head of doctrine is assuredly correct in its statements that "The death of the Son of God . . . is of infinite worth and value . . . because the person who submitted to it was not only really man and perfectly holy, but also the only-begotten Son of God."[15] The price paid by Jesus on the cross is incalculable because it was a price paid *both* by the one perfect, holy representative of humanity as a whole and Israel in particular, *and* by the only-begotten Son of God.

The significance of Jesus' blood being shed was not lost on the writers of the letter to the Hebrews. The sacrifices of the blood of goats and calves had only temporary effect, but Jesus' blood secured eternal redemption (Heb 9:12).

How was this so? On the one hand, "Only the death of the Son at the outermost extreme of human depravity and divine self-abandonment is commensurate with the gravity and power of Sin."[16] On the other hand, there is no strict equivalence between

---

14. Roberts and Wilson, *Echoes of Exodus*, 30.
15. "Synod of Dort."
16. Rutledge, *The Crucifixion*, 292.

Redemption and the Cost of Salvation

the size of the debt incurred to God by sinful human beings and the price paid by God himself to redeem us.

Steve Holmes suggests that sin is like pollution.[17] In the summer of 2020, there was a catastrophic oil spillage in Mauritius, caused when the MV Wakashio ran aground. Sin, like pollution, destroys lives, stains, weighs down and entangles, and damages whole systems. Jesus' death was, in the infinite, unfathomable wisdom of the Triune God, the cost of cleaning up the entire ecosystem and all the creatures in it.

God did not weigh up exactly how much was needed to pay off the debts of our enslavement; God made the ultimate sacrifice in order to do far more than merely wipe them out. This is because "*In Jesus, it is the triune God himself* who has intervened to reclaim—to buy back, if you will—his lost creation, and the price he pays is his own self in the person of the divine Son of Man."[18]

The cost of our salvation is incalculable, so far exceeding the totality of the national debt countries have built up fighting the coronavirus that it is in a wholly different league. But even so, God overpaid in order to save us. P. T. Forsyth imagines God the Father saying:

> Do you stumble at the cost? It has cost Me more than if the price paid were all Mankind. For it cost Me My only and beloved Son to justify My name or righteousness, and to realise the destiny of My creature in holy love. And all mankind is not so great and dear as He. Nor is its suffering the enormity in a moral world that His Cross is. I am no spectator in the course of things, and no speculator on the result. I spared not My own Son. We carried the load that crushes you. It bowed Him into the ground. On the third day He rose with a new creation in His hand, and a regenerate world, and all things working together for good to love and the holy purpose in love. And what He did I did. How I did it? How I do it? This

---

17. Holmes, *The Wondrous Cross*, 94.
18. Rutledge, *The Crucifixion*, 294.

you know not now, and could not, but you shall know hereafter.[19]

Jesus died as Son of God and Son of Man. As Son of God, the price he paid was incalculable. As Son of Man, the price he paid was representative. He was the pure lamb, whose sacrifice was accepted as covering over the sins of the world. As we have already seen in our discussion of compounding, when a sacrifice was made, the offering was accepted on behalf of the whole. In 1 Corinthians 15, Paul applies that logic to the resurrection. He describes Jesus Christ as the firstfruits of those who have died (verse 20). Jesus' death, offered as a sacrifice to God, is thoroughly effective. Just as "in Adam all die, so in Christ all will be made alive" (verse 22). Because Jesus was raised from the dead, we can be confident that when he returns again, "those who belong to him" will be resurrected (verse 23). All the powers of evil will be destroyed, ending with the extinction of death itself (verses 25–26).

Jesus paid the price as our surety

When my daughter was a student and wanted to rent a flat, I had to give a guarantee that if she did not pay her rent, I would. A person who gives a guarantee is called a surety, because their promise gives assurance to the recipient that the money owed will be paid. But, depending on the wording used in the legal documents, a surety can do more than simply pay compensation if the primary debtor fails to pay up. A surety can promise to render the performance instead of the primary debtor. The kinsman-redeemer is a special case of a surety.

Jesus took on the full range of obligations to act as our surety. The idea that Jesus was our surety is a prominent theme in the writings of Puritans such as John Owen and Richard Sibbes. Owen saw Jesus as our surety, the one who gave the Father the faithful, trusting, and obedient love which every human being owed God. Jesus is the one who makes up for our failure to pay our debt to

---

19. Forsyth, *Justification*, 169–70.

God; Jesus not only pays the price we have incurred because of our disobedience and rejection of God's love; Jesus is also the one who gives God the love and obedience we should have given God.

Eighteenth-century American theologian Jonathan Edwards described Jesus Christ as our surety and our representative in his "Discourse on Justification." As our surety and representative, Jesus has done on our behalf all that God the Father asked him to do and who kept all of God's commands perfectly.

> Indeed the justification of a believer is no other than his being admitted to communion in the justification of this head and surety of all believers; for as Christ suffered the punishment of sin, not as a private person, but as our surety; so when after this suffering he was raised from the dead, he was therein justified, not as a private person, but as the surety and representative of all that should believe in him. So that he was raised again not only for his own, but also for our justification, according to the apostle, Rom. iv. 25.[20]

Jesus acts as our surety both as our kinsman-redeemer and as our representative. In his death, Jesus represented not only each one of us as individuals but also the human race as a whole. As P. T. Forsyth put it, "The Son of God was not an individual merely; He was the representative of the whole race, and its *vis-à-vis*, on its own scale."[21]

The idea of Jesus as our surety is very close to the idea that Jesus recapitulates the story of humanity in general and Israel in particular. The apostle Paul in Romans 5:12–21 describes Jesus as the Second Adam. Irenaeus, bishop of Lyons (c. 130–202 AD), developed the idea of recapitulation by comparing the careers of Adam and Jesus. Whereas the path of sinful humanity is summed up and exemplified in the disobedience of Adam to God's commands in the garden of Eden, the path of redeemed humanity is summed up and exemplified in the obedience of Jesus to God's commands in the garden of Gethsemane. Where Adam

---

20. Edwards, "Discourse," 1:623.
21. Forsyth, *The Work of Christ*, 116.

was disobedient concerning God's command concerning the fruit of the tree of knowledge, Jesus was obedient through his death on the wood of a tree.[22] The idea of recapitulation can be developed further: where the people of Israel wandered in the desert for forty years because of their rejection of God's word spoken through Moses; Jesus endured forty days of temptation in the desert through his commitment to the Torah.

An anonymous early Christian writer wrote in a sermon about Jesus' baptism, "Even as he fulfilled the righteousness of baptism, he fulfilled also the righteousness of being born and growing, of eating and drinking, of sleeping and relaxing. He also fulfilled the righteousness of experiencing temptation, fear, flight, and sadness, as well as suffering, death, and resurrection: that is, according to the requirement of the human nature he took upon himself, he fulfilled all these acts of righteousness."[23]

For Irenaeus, Jesus' recapitulation of the human condition includes the cancellation of the debt to God which humanity incurred by eating the forbidden fruit from the tree of the knowledge of good and evil. The original sin of disobeying God took place at a tree; the ground of our forgiveness depended on Jesus' obedience unto death on a wooden cross, "so that as by means of a tree we were made debtors to God, [so also] by means of a tree we may obtain the remission of our debt."[24]

Where Adam, the father of humanity, and all who have followed him have failed to live lives pleasing to God, Jesus alone lived a life of consistent, coherent, obedient love for the Father.

Hans Boersma is among the many theologians who find Irenaeus's idea helpful. Boersma says:

> As the representative of Israel and Adam, Christ instructs us and models for us the love of God (moral influence). As the representative of Israel and Adam, Christ suffers God's judgment on evil and bears the suffering of the curse of the law (penal representation). As

---

22. Boersma, *Heavenly Participation*, 41–44.
23. Anonymous, "Incomplete Work on Matthew," 46.
24. Irenaeus, *Against Heresies* V.17.2.

the representative of Israel and Adam, Christ fights the powers of evil, expels demons, withstands satanic temptation to the point of death, and rises victorious from the grave (Christus Victor).[25]

To whom was the price of our redemption paid?

The previous chapter looked at the idea of Christ's death as a ransom. We discovered that there are problems with thinking of the ransom as having been paid to the devil and also with the idea that the ransom was paid to God. We saw that Gregory of Nazianus was wise to suggest that it isn't helpful to try to find an answer to the question, To whom was the ransom paid?

If we think about Christ's death as our redemption from slavery, similar problems arise. Slavery was widespread in the ancient world. Genesis 34 describes how Joseph's brothers, envious that Joseph was their father's most beloved son, sold him to Ishmaelite traders on their way to Egypt. Some philosophers thought that because slavery was everywhere, it must be part of the way the world was made. Aristotle said that some human beings were slaves because all they were fit for was to be used as living tools by others. Other philosophers recognized that slavery was always unnatural. Some (but by no means all) of the early church fathers got muddled because they accepted that because slavery was lawful under Roman law, it was just. So Gregory of Nyssa (d. 385 AD) argued that "if any one out of regard for the person who has so sold himself should use violence against him who has bought him, he will clearly be acting unjustly in thus arbitrarily rescuing one who has been legally purchased as a slave."[26] As lawyers and many others know, the fact that something is lawful is by no means a guarantee that it is just.

Hans Boersma cautions us:

---

25. Boersma, *Violence, Hospitality and the Cross*, 112–13.
26. Gregory of Nyssa, *The Great Catechism*.

> Metaphors are pressed too far . . . when we expand or generalize their application. This happens, for instance, when we use the commercial metaphor of redemption (the freeing of slaves by means of payment) to argue that it is the devil or God the Father who demands payment. Such generalizing does not take into account the limited scope of the metaphor.[27]

The implications of our redemption

As we have seen, in the Hebrew Scriptures, the redemption of Israel from Egypt is remembered as a demonstration of God's power and God's judgment on oppressors (Exod 6:6; Deut 9:26; 2 Sam 7:23; 1 Chr 17:2; Ps 77:15; 78:42; 106:10–12). But it is also understood as a purchase, as God buying back his inheritance (Ps 74:2).

Christ's redemption of us is not merely setting us free from slavery to sin. Christ himself *is* our redemption (1 Cor 1:30). "We have redemption in Christ only because he has redeemed us to be his possession."[28]

God our heavenly Father does not let us loose; he adopts us as his children. Paul makes this clear in Galatians 4. Christ came "to redeem those under the law, that we might receive adoption to sonship" (Gal 4:5). Our redemption transforms who we are. The certificate of indebtedness recording our sin is destroyed; we are given a certificate of freedom from slavery and, even more importantly, a certificate that we have been adopted as children of God. Our adoption as God's children is sealed by the Holy Spirit who God the Father and God the Son have sent into our hearts (Gal 4:6).

Our redemption is about God buying back God's inheritance, it is about us coming into our inheritance as God's adopted children, and it is about God calling us to live in ways which avoid falling back into slavery.

---

27. Boersma, *Violence, Hospitality and the Cross*, 107.
28. Torrance, *Atonement*, 180.

Redemption and the Cost of Salvation

In 1 Corinthians 7:23, Paul challenges those who are free to think of themselves as Christ's slaves, advising them that "you were bought with a price; do not become slaves of human beings." As Richard B. Hays says in his commentary on 1 Corinthians, the metaphor being used is of slaves being purchased from the slave market by a new master.[29] In the same way as God's redemption of the Israelites from Egypt meant that they belonged to him, so too our redemption from sin and death means that we belong to Jesus. We are to serve the one who has paid the price to buy us back from the powers that oppress us and from the consequences of the choices we have made.

The Long Psalm prays for redemption from the oppression of men, so that the Psalmist can obey God's commands (Ps 119:134). In Isaiah 48:17, God reminds God's people that he is "your Redeemer, the Holy One of Israel . . . who teaches you what is best for you, who directs you in the way you should go."

As we will explore further in the final chapter, God, who has redeemed us with justice and righteousness (Isa 1:27), calls us to live lives worthy of him, lives characterized by love, faith, hope, holiness, purity, and justice. This idea is made explicit in Titus 2:14, where Paul says that our God and Savior Jesus Christ "gave himself for us to redeem us from all wickedness and to purify for himself a people that are his very own, eager to do what is good." The redeemed of the Lord are to be a holy people (Isa 62:12).

Conclusion

Redemption, like ransom, highlights that we are captives. But redemption emphasizes the extent to which our captivity is the result of our own choices and warns that its end result will be death. Our only hope is if our burden of debt is somehow lifted. We will explore that further in the next chapter.

If we are redeemed, someone needed to pay the price. That someone needed to take the place of the sacrificial lamb, to be the

---

29. Hays, *First Corinthians*, 106.

firstborn, to be free from the captivity to sin and the liability to death which face us, and to be able to act as our kinsman-redeemer. Jesus was all of these things and more. We have been redeemed as a result of Jesus' life of holy, faithful, trusting, obedient, love for God the Father.

The idea of redemption has its roots in the experience of slaves. Today, there are few countries in the world where slavery is officially lawful. There are, however, many, many people trapped in slavery, whether trapped making mud bricks, or working in a sweatshop, or trafficked for sex. These people are in need of both physical and spiritual redemption. But everyone needs rescuing from evil, sin, and death.

> Lamb of God, who takes away the sin of the world, look on us and have mercy on us, you who are both victim and priest, reward and redeemer; keep safe from all evils those whom you have redeemed, O Savior of the world.[30]

---

30. Anonymous, "Old Gallican Missal."

Forgiveness and the Debt to God

Stories of forgiveness

WE'VE BEGUN PREVIOUS CHAPTERS with contemporary stories of kidnapping victims being ransomed and of slaves being redeemed. Finding a story of debts being truly forgiven is much harder. There are three levels of debt forgiveness: a creditor forgoing the interest on a debt, a creditor agreeing to accept less than the full sum lent, and a creditor writing off the entirety of the debt.

Examples of creditors forgoing the interest on a debt are commonplace. What the creditor is doing here is agreeing to give up some of the profit they were expecting to make from a loan in exchange for the borrower repaying the sum borrowed. Relatively often, a creditor will take the view that so long as they get back the sum they lent they haven't lost out on the deal, and if the borrower is able to pay part of the interest, that will be enough to enable both sides to move on. A lot of the debt forgiveness offered by rich countries and their banks to the developing world was really this sort of arrangement, writing off a sum of interest which all sides had long ago realized was never going to be repaid.

When it is obvious that a borrower cannot repay the loan in full, a creditor may agree to accept less than the sum they lent. This is painful for a creditor. The creditor is not just giving up some of the profit they were expecting to make; they are accepting a loss on the loan. This sort of arrangement is known in the financial services sector as "taking a haircut." Creditors agree to it if they think they are faced with a choice between getting some of the money back now or risking getting even less of it back later.

In February 2020, the IMF warned bondholders of Argentina's national debt that the country's debt burden was unsustainable, and that bondholders needed to accept reductions in the $100 billion Argentina owed ($44 billion of which was owed to the IMF itself).

Neither a reduction in the interest owed nor a haircut on the sum lent are full debt forgiveness. Full debt forgiveness only occurs when a creditor writes off the entirety of a loan. Full debt forgiveness transforms the nature of the transaction, changing it from a loan into a gift. That is why full debt forgiveness is so rare. When it occurs, the creditors bear the entirety of the cost.

After World War I, the victorious powers decided that the defeated countries, principally Germany, should pay for the costs of the war. The costs, called "reparations," were set at such a high level that by 1923 the German economy could not keep up with the repayments. The misery and resentment that reparations caused the German people were part of the conditions which allowed the Nazi Party's rise to power.

After World War II, in contrast, the Western Allied powers introduced a currency reform in Germany. This left basic business debts and employer debts to employees in place, but otherwise all debts were cancelled on the basis that most were owed to former Nazis. This Year of Jubilee, and the absence of any reparations payable to the Allied powers, enabled West Germany to recover from the effects of the World Wars and prosper.

Because full debt forgiveness turns a loan into a gift, it hardly ever happens outside of family relationships. In the Canadian television comedy-drama *Republic of Doyle*, Jake Doyle has recently discovered that he has a sixteen-year-old daughter called Sloan. She runs away, but not before emptying all the family's savings and stealing from an organized crime boss, Vick Saul. Jake's biggest concern is the safety of his daughter rather than the financial problems she has caused. When she is found by Saul's men, Jake not only forgives her the loss of the family's savings, he also takes on the burden of repaying her debt to the mobster.

Being in debt

We are all in debt. Our condition is not just that of being in debt; we are beings in debt. But there are different kinds of debt. There are debts of gratitude, financial debts (both collective and personal), and there are debts of guilt.

Debts of gratitude

The debt to God

John S. Pobee makes the important point that "precisely because we are each and all God's creation and children, we are each and all debtors to God (Matt 18:23–35) who makes his rain fall on the just and the unjust."[1] We are indebted to God from the moment that we are born and for every good thing that we enjoy.

The debt which every human being owes God is like the debt human children owe their parents. It is not primarily a debt of obedience, though it involves obedience. It is, at heart, a debt of gratitude, an obligation to be thankful to those whose love has brought us into being and whose care has sustained and nurtured us. We owe to God our very selves.

The introduction to the Ten Commandments in the Book of Exodus reminds the Israelites that "I am the Lord your God who has delivered you out of slavery in Egypt" (Exod 20:2). The Ten Commandments begin with commands declaring that God is the one to whom we are to give thanks for good harvests, for work, for fertility, for shelter, and for protection.

The New Testament similarly reminds us that we owe everything to God. Every relationship, every gift, every talent, every

---

1. Pobee, "The Ethics of Debt," 68.

ability, the health we enjoy in our body, every good thing that we have comes from God (Jas 1:17). What God has given us freely God has every right to take away. Everything that we have is repayable on demand.

Even if we never sinned, we would still owe God a debt of worship, of praise and thankfulness for life and all the other good gifts that God has given us. That is why the angels, who have never sinned, worship God constantly, proclaiming God to be holy and thanking God for the life God has given them (Isa 6:3; Rev 4:8).

In Luke 12:13–21, Jesus tells the story of the rich farmer who was investing for his future, looking forward to his comfortable retirement, perhaps in the equivalent of Florida or in the south of France. The problem was that he had forgotten that God could, at any moment, demand his life. Instead of seeing his life as a gift from God to be used in the service of others, he had treated it as his own property and had spent it (again a financial metaphor) in pursuit of his own comfort and pleasures.

The debt to our parents and to previous generations

In the Ten Commandments, the commands concerned with the exclusive worship of God are followed by the commandment to honor your father and mother. In the ancient Middle East, as in many places in the world even today, good parenting regularly included making sure that it was you, rather than your children, who went to bed hungry. Good parenting involves nurturing, providing for, and making sacrifices for one's children. Those of us who were brought up by nonabusive parents have much to thank them for.

Tribal and Eastern cultures are conscious of the debt we owe to previous generations. The computer equipment enabling me to write this book depends on the discoveries of scientists stretching back to Michael and Sarah Faraday and beyond. The comparatively stable democratic institutions and relatively (despite significant failures) just laws which I enjoy as a citizen of the United Kingdom are something I owe to those who fought for them over the course of nearly one thousand years. Edmund Burke was absolutely right to insist that, however much things are in need of reform, we all owe a debt of gratitude to those who are responsible for the good things in our cultural and national heritage.[2]

Financial debts, both collective and personal

National indebtedness

Our solidarity with other human beings does not only give rise to debts of gratitude. Elettra Stimilli writes that "today, more than ever, 'being in debt' does not indicate a state in which one enters at any given moment in life, but is the original state in which everyone is born, poor or wealthy . . . states transmit their debt to those who are part of it even before they are born."[3] In many countries, each generation is born into a situation in which they will be paying the national debt incurred during previous generations. Whether it is the cost of wars, vanity projects by politicians, pension liabilities, bailing out banks, or the enormous debts countries have incurred in fighting the COVID-19 pandemic, each us carries the load of debt for which we are liable but not responsible. Financial debt is not only something which results from our individual choices; it is also a world-system in which we are trapped.

That was true, for example, for the people of the Democratic Republic of the Congo (DRC, formerly Zaire). Despite the fact that Erwin Blumenthal reported to the IMF's managing director in 1980 that the central bank of Zaire was utterly corrupt and rotten, that no creditor could ever expect to get their money back, the IMF, the World Bank, and the British and American governments lent President Mobuto of Zaire $8.5 billion between 1981 and 1990. The people of the Democratic Republic of the Congo were left with crippling debts, compounded by an economic crisis which saw GDP per capita halve between 1990 and 2000. The World Bank reports that in 2018, 72 percent of the DRC's population were living

---

2. Burke, *Reflections on the Revolution in France*, 117.
3. Stimilli, *Debt and Guilt*, 159–60.

in extreme poverty on less than $1.90 a day, and 43 percent of its children are malnourished.

The DRC is not alone in its predicament. "According to the United Nations, developing countries paid $1.662 trillion in servicing debt between the years 1980 and 1992—three times the original amount owed in 1980. What is even more staggering is that despite this repayment, the total debt of developing countries is still estimated at more than $1.3 trillion."[4]

George Carey, writing for Christian Aid in *Proclaim Liberty*, published in 1998, feared that "More children could die unnecessary deaths before the year 2000 as a result of the debt crisis that enslaves poor countries today than were killed in passage during the infamous Atlantic slave trade. For every second that passes, another child is born into unpayable debt in the world's poorest countries. From Mozambique to Tanzania . . . more is spent on servicing external debt than on either education or health."[5]

But national indebtedness is not a phenomenon unique to the developing world. To be born as a child in the Republic of Ireland is to inherit the debt which the Irish government incurred when, on September 30, 2008, it took the unprecedented step of giving an explicit guarantee of €400 billion of deposits, loans, bonds, and senior and subordinated debt owed by banks in the country. This represented a potential commitment of €97,560 per head of the Irish population, and more than twice Ireland's gross domestic product! In the event, the guarantee actually cost €64 billion, but this still loaded every Irish adult and child with a debt of more than €15,000 each.

As we have seen, even today, debt is imposed on the children of debtors. Each child who becomes an adult citizen inherits the national debt which previous governments have incurred. In the case of developing countries, children whose parents grew up under ravenous dictators are deprived of education and health care as tax revenues are diverted to pay interest to foreign banks, investors, and countries. In the West, children have inherited pension

4. Ndundgane, "Seizing the New Millennium," 26.
5. Carey, "Chains around Africa," 16.

liabilities and the costs of government bailouts during the global financial crisis. All around the world, our children and grandchildren will bear the cost of combatting COVID-19 and of trying to halt the destruction of the planet which the self-centered lifestyles of those like myself, used to comfort and convenience, have caused.

Personal indebtedness

I do worry about how my children's generation will manage under the burden of the debts and liabilities which the Baby Boomers and my Generation X have imposed on them. But what keeps me awake at night are the debts I have incurred personally. Unpayable debts destroy families.

One of my close friends, Rob Horner, is a barrister who used to do family law cases. One of the saddest cases he ever dealt with involved a divorcing couple who were arguing not about how to divide up the family's assets but about which of them should be responsible for the mountain of debt they had run up. The tragedy was that not only was their debt unpayable, their continued arguments were only increasing its size (lawyers have to be paid, after all!). Both were bankrupt; their efforts to avoid it were only making the debt worse.[6]

Even those of us who have our debts under control should be aware of their weight. The largest financial debt many of us will ever take on is called a mortgage. The word is made up of two French words: *mort*, meaning death, and *gage*, meaning pledge or bargain. A mortgage is literally a bargain with death. To mortgage a property was to hand ownership of that property over to a creditor; unless the loan was repaid, the property was lost.

Debts of guilt

To be guilty is to owe a debt. We can see this most clearly when we think about theft. When we steal something which belongs to

---

6. Horner, "The Beatitudes for Lawyers."

another, we owe a debt, a debt to return the thing we have stolen and a debt to atone for having stolen it. Philosophers such as Aristotle sometimes extrapolate from this that criminal acts should be thought of as taking more than is due to us and that we are therefore obliged to pay back what we have taken in order to restore the balance to society.

This link between debt and guilt is even more obvious in German. The German word *Schuld* means both "guilt" and "debt." In 1917 a German translation of Fyodor Dostoyevsky's novel *Crime and Punishment* was published under the title *Schuld und Sühne* (*Guilt and Atonement*).

Moreover, as Nietzsche (one of Christianity's most informed critics) saw, human beings have, because of their sin, incurred "a debt . . . of such magnitude as only God himself, the creditor, could discharge."[7]

In fact, we are twice indebted to Jesus. Jesus is the Word of God through whom we were created (John 1:3); Jesus is also the Lamb of God who rescued us from death (John 1:29). We owe God both a never-ending debt of gratitude and an unpayable debt of guilt. Our guilt before God makes us debtors to God; our guilt towards one another makes us debtors to our neighbors. And that debt, if not repaid, leads to captivity and death.

Imprisonment for debt

In the chapter on redemption we looked at debt leading to slavery. An alternative to debt-slavery was the debtor's prison. In the ancient Greek and Roman worlds, debt was the most common reason for imprisonment. Minor crimes (misdemeanors) were punished by a fine or some form of humiliation. Major crimes (felonies) were punished by enslavement or execution. It was primarily for failure to pay your debts that you ended up in prison.

The thinking behind putting a debtor in prison was, first, if the debtor had any hidden assets, the debtor would quickly make

---

7. Bentley Hart, *The Beauty of the Infinite*, 101.

arrangements to sell them in order to purchase their freedom; second, if the debtor could not buy their own way out of prison, their imprisonment would put pressure on their family and friends to pay their debt in order to secure their release. This would have been particularly effective in Palestine, where the law of Moses identified family members who had specific responsibility to redeem their kin from debt-slavery (Lev 25:7–49).

Imprisonment for debt was a long-standing feature of English law, formally abolished in the 1860s (though subject to important exceptions, some of which still exist today). Even in the first decade of the twentieth century, nearly ten thousand people were sentenced to imprisonment for failing to pay a judgment debt.

Like nineteenth-century Britons who could all recognize the description of debtors' prison in Charles Dickens's novels, first-century Jews would all have known of someone imprisoned by the Roman authorities for not paying their taxes or for not repaying a debt to a powerful money-lender. When Jesus read from Isaiah 61 in the synagogue, he announced that he had been sent to proclaim release to the captives. The first thing his audience would have thought of was not spiritual oppression but the all-too-material experience of being confined in a smelly, unhealthy Roman jail.

In England, the implications of being indebted have changed radically in the last century and a half. Well into the nineteenth century, criminals were usually only held in prisons awaiting trial or execution. The long-term inhabitants of prisons were mainly debtors. If you did not pay your debts, your creditors could have you imprisoned until you did so. The great nineteenth-century author Charles Dickens had personal experience of the practice of imprisonment for debt: his own father had been confined in the Marshalsea Prison in 1824 for failing to repay a debt of £40.

Biographer Claire Tomalin says that

> Charles, . . . just twelve years old, was sent out to a pawnbroker in the Hampstead Road, first with the books he loved, then with items of furniture, until after a few weeks the house was almost empty and the family was camping out in two bare rooms in the cold weather. All

these experiences—of debt, fear, angry creditors, bailiffs, pawnbrokers, prison, living in freezing empty rooms and managing on what can be borrowed or begged—were impressed on his mind and used again and again in his stories and novels, sometimes grimly, sometimes with humor.[8]

Once everything that could be sold had been sold, Dickens, aged twelve, had had to go work in a factory manufacturing shoe blacking. The 2017 film *The Man Who Invented Christmas* suggests that this experience continued to haunt Dickens.

The Pickwick Papers and *David Copperfield*

Dickens describes life for debtors inside the Marshalsea and the Fleet prisons in several of his novels.

In the light-hearted *Pickwick Papers* (1836–37), he lampoons the absurdity of the system. Mr. Pickwick's landlady, Mrs. Bardell, is urged by her lawyers, Dodson and Fogg, to sue Mr. Pickwick for breaching an alleged promise to marry her. A jury finds Mr. Pickwick liable and orders him to pay damages of £750 plus costs. Mr. Pickwick is outraged, since he never intended to make Mrs. Bardell any offer of marriage. When Mr. Pickwick is arrested for not paying the judgment, he is taken to the Fleet Prison. Mr. Pickwick now faces the prospect of a lifetime in prison if he continues with his stubborn refusal to pay the unjust judgment. There he remains until Dodson and Fogg have Mrs. Bardell thrown into the same prison for not paying their bill for the costs of the litigation. At this point, Mr. Pickwick is prevailed upon to pay off Dodson and Fogg if Mrs. Bardell agrees to abandon her claim for the judgment debt. Mr. Pickwick and Mrs. Bardell are released, and everyone lives happily ever after.

In *David Copperfield* (1849–50), Mr. Micawber, the eternal optimist (modeled on Dickens's own father), explains the knife-edge that people walked. Mr. Micawber has been imprisoned in

8. Tomalin, *Dickens*, 23.

the King's Bench prison for debt. When David Copperfield goes to visit him, Mr. Micawber tells him "that if a man had twenty pounds for his income, and spent nineteen pounds nineteen shillings and sixpence, he would be happy, but that if he spent twenty pounds one [shilling] he would be miserable."[9]

The prisons where the debtors were confined were run for profit. Conditions inside were grotesque. For those with a means of income or good contacts, private rooms could be rented within the prison. Family could come to live with them and friends were free to visit regularly. David Copperfield says that because of the help they received from friends and relatives, Mr. and Mrs. Micawber "lived more comfortably in the prison than they had lived for a long while out of it." For those with access to funds, prisons were like an overpriced hotel which it could be worth staying in if you wanted desperately to avoid ever having to repay your creditors.

Despite the humorous tone of *The Pickwick Papers*, Dickens uses the opportunity to bring to his readers' attention the very different fates which awaited the well-connected and the poor inside a debtors' prison. In chapter XLI, Pickwick sees a number of holes in the ground which he thinks are for storing coal. He is told that people live and die in those "wretched dungeons." He is then led upstairs to a room "containing eight or nine iron bedsteads" which is comparatively comfortable, even if Mr. Pickwick is not convinced when the warden says that it is better than the Farringdon Hotel.

As Mr. Pickwick comes to understand the system in the prison, he realizes that, if he has money available to him, he can rent a single room. The prisoner whose room he takes "had been there long enough to have lost friends, fortune, home, and happiness." The man tells Mr. Pickwick:

> I could not be more forgotten or unheeded than I am here. I am a dead man; dead to society, without the pity they bestow on those whose souls have passed to judgment . . . I have sunk from the prime of life into old age, in this place, and there is not one to raise his hand above

---

9. Dickens, *David Copperfield*, 138.

my bed when I lie dead upon it, and say, "It is a blessing he is gone!"[10]

Despite being a prison for debtors, everything given to the inmates had to be paid for. Charitable gifts only paid for an inadequate amount of food for the poor debtors. Dickens was appalled:

> We still leave unblotted in the leaves of our statute book, for the reverence and admiration of succeeding ages, the just and wholesome law which declares that the sturdy felon shall be fed and clothed, and that the penniless debtor shall be left to die of starvation and nakedness. This is no fiction. Not a week passes over our heads, but, in every one of our prisons for debt, some of these men must inevitably expire in the slow agonies of want.[11]

Dickens describes Mr. Pickwick walking past as series of poor wretches, the last of whom is his acquaintance, Mr. Job Trotter. Mr. Pickwick invites Mr. Trotter to walk in the open air with him. He then asks Mr. Trotter why he isn't wearing a coat. Mr. Trotter explains how he has been forced to pawn the very clothes he wears in order to pay for food in the prison. "Gone, my dear sir—last coat—can't help it. Lived on a pair of boots—whole fortnight. Silk umbrella—ivory handle—week."

One of the warders, Mr. Jingle, then describes the future awaiting Job Trotter.

> Nothing soon—lie in bed—starve—die—Inquest—little bone-house—poor prisoner—common necessities—hush it up—gentlemen of the jury—warden's tradesmen—keep it snug—natural death—coroner's order—workhouse funeral—serve him right—all over—drop the curtain.[12]

Mr. Jingle's prediction was not hyperbole on Dickens's part. A century earlier, in 1729, a British Parliamentary Committee found that three hundred prisoners had died of starvation in a period of

---

10. Dickens, *The Pickwick Papers*, 476.
11. Dickens, *The Pickwick Papers*, 477.
12. Dickens, *The Pickwick Papers*, 478.

three months, and that every day between eight and ten prisoners died because of hot weather.

Little Dorrit

The debtors' prison at the Marshalsea is the main location for the first half of the book, *Little Dorrit* (1855–56). It is set in the 1820s, the time when Dickens's own father had been imprisoned for debt. Little Dorrit's father has become completely institutionalized in the Marshalsea prison. Little Dorrit is born and grows up in the prison. A child of a slave would be enslaved from birth. Although Little Dorrit was not a slave, the shape of her childhood was determined by her father's indebtedness. As a twelve-year-old boy, Charles Dickens himself had inherited the responsibility for working to repay his father's debt. In a similar way, Little Dorrit supports her family through her sewing, though without hope of ever earning enough to repay it.

Little Dorrit is a Christ-like figure. Claire Tomalin describes her as displaying "a persistent goodness that shines out over the shabby world through which she moves, and to which she contributes her practical skills, her hard work, and her kindness to those more unfortunate than herself."[13] When, after his release from prison, her corrupt father "behaves cruelly and shamefully towards her," she continues to give him "unconditional love and support."[14]

The nineteenth century had a much greater sense of the solidarity of debt than we do today. As Dickens's writings show, a debtor's fate affected the lives of their immediate family, and gave rise to feelings of moral obligation on the part of their wider family and friends.

---

13. Tomalin, *Dickens*, 259.
14. Tomalin, *Dickens*, 263.

Ransomed, Redeemed, and Forgiven

Imprisonment for debt after Charles Dickens

By highlighting the conditions in the debtors' prisons, Charles Dickens's novels changed the public mood. In 1869, imprisonment for debt in most cases was abolished by the Debtors Act. However, it did remain in certain circumstances. Despite the Debtors Act in 1869, imprisonment for debt has not been completely abolished. In 2020, the English Court of Appeal confirmed that someone who has made sworn promises (called "undertakings") to a court that they will repay a debt can be sent to prison for not keeping those promises: Hussain v. Vaswani (2020) EWCA Civ 1216. A few years earlier, I had appeared in court for an eighty-one-year-old man who had been ordered by a court to share the divide the profits from a family company with his brother. Instead of obeying the court order, he had transferred the money (around £450,000) to Hong Kong. Despite the judge giving him every opportunity to repay the money, he refused to do so. Eventually, the judge felt he had no option but to sentence my client to prison. The national newspapers in the UK carried headlines of my client being taken, in his wheelchair, into the prison van.

Recognizing that we are in debt

Remembering our debts of gratitude

In the Western world, while we are constantly conscious of our financial debts, we have forgotten our debts of gratitude and we seek to deny our debts of guilt.

We can approach the world in two very different ways: we can think that the world owes us a living or we can acknowledge that everything good that we enjoy in the world is the result of the work of others. The American revolutionary Thomas Paine is a key source of the belief that modern Western human beings have that the world owes them a living. In his book the *Rights of Man*, published in 1791 in the middle of the French Revolution, he wrote,

Forgiveness and the Debt to God

"Society grants [the citizen] nothing. Every man is a proprietor in society, and draws on the capital as a matter of right."[15]

Philosopher Roger Scruton says that Paine's ideas have led to an emphasis on "my rights," which has become, in the guise of human rights, a religion. The central creed of this "secular religion of human rights" is "that we owe the world nothing, and that the world owes everything to us." As a result, "We kill in ourselves both piety and gratitude."[16]

Our culture teaches our children first about their rights rather than their responsibilities; about their entitlements rather than their duties; about their freedom to do what they want rather than the reasons why they should live virtuously.

Acknowledgment of the ways we are indebted to others is profoundly countercultural. It is no longer normal to say "grace," a prayer of thanks to God before eating a meal. The practice of writing thank you letters in response to birthday and Christmas presents is dying out. Our culture has become so used to getting everything "on demand" and remotely that we have fewer incentives and opportunities to express gratitude to those who serve and provide for us.

There are three key figures in the parable Jesus tells in Luke 15:11–32. There is the prodigal son, the generous father, and the resentful brother. The true debt-slave in the parable of the prodigal son is, contrary to first appearances, his resentful brother. The prodigal son is reconciled to the generous father once he has acknowledged that he has sinned against him and is not worthy to be called his son (Luke 15:21). That reconciliation brings out into the open his brother's resentment of all the years he has spent slaving for the father (Luke 15:29). But the father is no slave-master; the resentful brother's slavery is of his own making. The resentful brother has failed to live the life of grateful enjoyment of the good gifts his father had always wanted to share with him.

---

15. Paine, *The Rights of Man*, 120.
16. Scruton, "Regaining my Religion."

Ransomed, Redeemed, and Forgiven

Acknowledging our debts of guilt

Contemporary Western culture promotes the idea that self-esteem is a key to good mental health. P. T. Forsyth argued that acknowledging that we are guilty is key to our spiritual health.[17] If our sense of self-worth, security, and identity is based on our self-esteem, how do we cope when we fail, fall short, or realize that we aren't up to it? If, by contrast, we find our sense of self-worth, security, and identity in the one who loved us despite the fact the debts of guilt that we have incurred, then we are on solid ground.

But only those who recognize that they are trapped and cannot rescue themselves can be ransomed. Only those who realize that they are enslaved can be redeemed. In order to discover God's forgiveness, we must acknowledge that we are not only in debt, we must accept that we are bankrupt. It is at the point where the prodigal son admits this that his journey home begins (Luke 15:17).

That is why Jesus says, "Blessed are the poor in spirit" (Matt 5:3). As Rob Horner explains:

> To be poor in spirit is to acknowledge that, before the Lord, we're not just spiritually in debt to Him; we're spiritually bankrupt. Our nature, and our continued actions, have run up a mountain of debt before Him that we have no hope of repaying. The Bible would say that, like the couple in my case, our daily actions actually continue to add to our debt—often, our deliberate actions serve only to make our debt worse.
>
> To be poor in spirit is to recognize that, before the Lord, on our own account, we are bankrupt, and there is nothing *we* can do about it.[18]

Our problem isn't just that we owe everything, our lives, our talents, our abilities, our wealth to God. Our problem is that we are behind on our installments. We are, in fact, hopelessly insolvent. As George Foot Moore says, "Man *owes* God obedience, and every

---

17. Forsyth, *The Work of Christ*, 78.
18. Horner, "The Beatitudes for Lawyers."

sin, whether or commission or omission, is a defaulted obligation, a debt."[19]

Debts that are repayable in installments usually contain acceleration clauses. An acceleration clause states that if the borrower is late in making one single payment, the whole amount borrowed is now repayable on demand. So, for example, if a borrower has taken out a ten-year loan, if they miss one installment in year three, the lender now has the right to ask the borrower to repay the whole of the outstanding sum borrowed. If that total sum is not paid, then the borrower's property and life may be forfeit.

This is the jolt Jesus delivers to the Pharisees and others who thought of their standing before God in terms of whether their good deeds outweighed the bad. We do not start life with a nil balance with God to which we can add by our good deeds and subtract by our bad deeds. We start life owing God everything. Any bad thing we do, say, or think is a missed installment, giving God every right to demand the immediate return of the whole of our life.

John Calvin understood the implications of this. In his *Commentary on 1 Timothy*, he wrote, "Since even the most perfect of us scarcely fulfill the hundredth part of their full duty, our liberality does not deserve to be taken into account before God; in fact if God called us to a full reckoning, there would be nobody who would avoid bankruptcy, so far are we from paying all that is due."[20]

Another picture might help. Holiness, covenant-faithfulness, is like a pure white sheet. Once there is a mark on the sheet, it is no longer pure white. Keeping the other parts of the sheet white does not remove the mark. Only washing the sheet removes the mark.

---

19. Moore, *Judaism in the First Centuries of the Christian Era*, 2:95.
20. Calvin, *Commentary on 1 Timothy*, 283.

The nature of forgiveness

No forgiveness without cost

It is a common mistake to think that forgiveness is free. It is not. Tim Keller tells a story about how one of his friends broke a chair which belonged to him. It did not matter whether the chair had been broken accidentally or deliberately, the fact is that the chair was broken. If the chair was to be repaired, someone had to pay for it. Either the friend would have to offer to pay to have the chair repaired or Tim would have had to pay for it himself. Either way, the chair had to be paid for before it could be repaired. The same is true of any debt. There is a cost to a debt which is forgiven; it is a cost borne by the person who does the forgiving.

In the first work Augustine wrote after he became bishop of Hippo, *Ad Simplicianum*, Augustine compares God with a creditor who has provide goods to a customer. By accepting the goods, the customer has incurred a debt. The customer owes repayment to the creditor. If the creditor decides to forgive the debt, the goods become a gift. The creditor has given up his right to repayment.[21]

Archbishop Desmond Tutu knew that forgiveness, although necessary to avoid a bloodbath in South Africa when the system of apartheid was dismantled, would be costly. So too did the French philosopher Jacques Derrida, in his work *On Cosmopolitanism and Forgiveness* (*OCF*). To forgive seems foolish. If I forgive you for hitting me in the face, what is to stop you deciding to hit me in the face again? J. K. A. Smith, commenting on Derrida's thought, says:

> To forgive is, in a sense, to welcome offence—to absorb a violation from another. As a result it is a kind of correlate or analogue of hospitality; and thus "pure" forgiveness must be *un*conditioned as absolute welcome . . . If forgiveness is ever *instrumental* to another desired good or end, then it is not "pure" forgiveness for Derrida. Pure forgiveness is an end in itself (*OCF*, 31–32).

---

21. Augustine, *Ad Simplicianum*.

Thus, Derrida announces an *axiom*: "Forgiveness forgives only the unforgivable" (*OCF*, 32).[22]

The things we can afford to forgive, the minor slights we can easily overlook, are not at the heart of what forgiveness demands. Forgiveness demands something much more costly, much more painful. As a result, J. K. A. Smith says, "If we forgive only the forgivable, then that's like the Pharisees who love only their friends (Matt 5). We are called to love our enemies, to forgive the unforgivable."[23]

Only someone who has truly had something unforgiveable to forgive can know what forgiveness really costs. When someone has wronged you, being merciful can often mean, on many levels, you bear the entire cost of their wrong. The cost of forgiving us is borne by God himself.

I have been to the death camps at Auschwitz twice. What I saw there the first time was unbelievable. Visiting the second time was even harder, knowing what traces of the horror and systematic dehumanization of over one million people (almost all of whom were Jews) lay in wait.

I have friends who have been to Rwanda, and seen the piles of bones left when 800,000 people (mostly Tutsis but also moderate Hutus who refused to participate in the killing) were put to death in just one hundred days in 1994.

I have visited Prishtina in Kosovo and been to the museum there which records the attacks by Serbian forces in the war in 1998–99. I have a very good friend there whose family members were killed during that conflict and whose bodies were marked by their killers with a cross to show that their killers were Orthodox Christians.

I have been affected by cases of rape and sexual assault far closer to home. A theology of forgiveness which pretends that there are no incidents of horrific, intolerable, inexplicable evil,

---

22. Smith, *Derrida*, 71.
23. Smith, *Derrida*, 71.

Ransomed, Redeemed, and Forgiven

and that forgiveness is cheap, easy, or without cost is thoroughly deluded.

Corrie ten Boom and her family risked their lives shielding Jews in Amsterdam during World War II. They were betrayed in February 1944, and Corrie and her sister Betsie were taken to Ravensbrück concentration camp. In the concentration camp, they were subject to the degradations the Nazis used in all their camps as a means of humiliating, demoralizing, and subduing their captives. Betsie died in the camp, but Corrie was released.

By 1946, Corrie was receiving speaking invitations to tell her story. In 1947, after she had spoken at a church in Munich, she was approached by a balding man in a gray overcoat step. Corrie froze. She knew this man well; he'd been one of the most vicious guards at Ravensbrück, one who had mocked the women prisoners as they showered. She describes what happened next:

> It came back with a rush: the huge room with its harsh overhead lights, the pathetic pile of dresses and shoes in the center of the floor, the shame of walking naked past this man. I could see my sister's frail form ahead of me, ribs sharp beneath the parchment skin. Betsie, how thin you were!
>
> Betsie and I had been arrested for concealing Jews in our home during the Nazi occupation of Holland; this man had been a guard at Ravensbrück concentration camp where we were sent.
>
> Now he was in front of me, hand thrust out: "A fine message, fräulein! How good it is to know that, as you say, all our sins are at the bottom of the sea!"
>
> And I, who had spoken so glibly of forgiveness, fumbled in my pocketbook rather than take that hand. He would not remember me, of course—how could he remember one prisoner among those thousands of women?
>
> But I remembered him and the leather crop swinging from his belt. It was the first time since my release that I had been face to face with one of my captors and my blood seemed to freeze.

"You mentioned Ravensbrück in your talk," he was saying. "I was a guard in there." No, he did not remember me.

"But since that time," he went on, "I have become a Christian. I know that God has forgiven me for the cruel things I did there, but I would like to hear it from your lips as well. Fräulein"—again the hand came out—"will you forgive me?"

And I stood there—I whose sins had every day to be forgiven—and could not. Betsie had died in that place—could he erase her slow terrible death simply for the asking?

It could not have been many seconds that he stood there, hand held out, but to me it seemed hours as I wrestled with the most difficult thing I had ever had to do.

For I had to do it—I knew that. The message that God forgives has a prior condition: that we forgive those who have injured us. "If you do not forgive men their trespasses," Jesus says, "neither will your Father in heaven forgive your trespasses."

I knew it not only as a commandment of God, but as a daily experience. Since the end of the war I had had a home in Holland for victims of Nazi brutality.

Those who were able to forgive their former enemies were able also to return to the outside world and rebuild their lives, no matter what the physical scars. Those who nursed their bitterness remained invalids. It was as simple and as horrible as that.

And still I stood there with the coldness clutching my heart. But forgiveness is not an emotion—I knew that too. Forgiveness is an act of the will, and the will can function regardless of the temperature of the heart.

"Jesus, help me!" I prayed silently. "I can lift my hand. I can do that much. You supply the feeling."

And so woodenly, mechanically, I thrust my hand into the one stretched out to me. And as I did, an incredible thing took place. The current started in my shoulder, raced down my arm, sprang into our joined hands. And then this healing warmth seemed to flood my whole being, bringing tears to my eyes.

"I forgive you, brother!" I cried. "With all my heart!"

Ransomed, Redeemed, and Forgiven

> For a long moment we grasped each other's hands, the former guard and the former prisoner. I had never known God's love so intensely as I did then. But even so, I realized it was not my love. I had tried, and did not have the power. It was the power of the Holy Spirit as recorded in Rom. 5:5: "because the love of God is shed abroad in our hearts by the Holy Spirit which is given unto us."[24]

Having stood by the gas chambers in Auschwitz, next to the rails where Jews arriving from all over Europe were sorted into those to be put to death immediately and those to be worked to death in the fields, makes the actions of Corrie ten Boom astonishing. The cost of forgiveness is not one we have the strength to pay ourselves; it is one we need the power of the Holy Spirit to be able to discharge.

"God calls us to forgive freely, to bear the cost and pain that forgiveness brings. And he does so only because he has done it first . . . precisely because God has borne the cost of forgiving us, he can ask us to bear the pain of forgiving one another."[25]

Forgiveness "is not easy, painless, or cheap, but it costs and hurts. And God's call on us to forgive, to love our enemies, is not easy and cheap, but will cost us and hurt us. The call, though, is to live as God lived, to bear the cost and pain ourselves."[26]

No forgiveness without justice

Just as we need to admit that we are captives before we can be ransomed, and we need to accept that we are slaves before we can be redeemed, so we need to acknowledge that we are bankrupt before we can be forgiven. Forgiveness goes beyond justice, but it does not bypass justice. As the parable of the prodigal son shows us, admitting our guilt/debt is the precondition for forgiveness. As Alasdair MacIntyre explains, the condition of forgiveness is that "the offender already accepts as just the verdict of the law upon his

---

24. Ten Boom, "I'm Still Learning To Forgive."
25. Holmes, *The Wondrous Cross*, 119.
26. Holmes, *The Wondrous Cross*, 110.

action and behaves as one who acknowledges the justice of the appropriate punishment . . . Justice is characteristically administered by a judge, by an impersonal authority representing the whole community; but forgiveness can only be extended by the offended party."[27]

The necessity for acceptance of the truth as the foundation of forgiveness is also made clear in Psalm 32. David says there, "Then I acknowledged my sin to you and did not cover up my iniquity. I said, 'I will confess my transgressions to the Lord'—and you forgive the guilt of my sin" (Ps 32:5). David had to admit that he had sinned and to bring it out into the open; only then could he be forgiven.

Archbishop Desmond Tutu understood that just as truth is indispensable to personal forgiveness, so truth is a necessary foundation for social reconstruction. That is why he insisted that the South African Truth and Reconciliation Commission would publish the truth about atrocities committed on all sides and would only grant amnesties on a case-by-case basis to those perpetrators who had admitted the full extent of their crimes.

Jesus' death as forgiveness of our debt to God

Jesus' life and death discharge our debts to God. As our surety, kinsman-redeemer and representative, Jesus fulfills our obligations to live lives of holy, faithful, trusting, obedient, love. On the cross, our debts of guilt are paid in full.

The certificate of indebtedness

The New American Standard Bible (NASB) translates Colossians 2:13–14 as follows:

> When you were dead in your transgressions and the uncircumcision of your flesh, He made you alive together with Him, having forgiven us all our transgressions,

27. MacIntyre, *After Virtue*, 174.

> having canceled out the certificate of debt (*cheirographon*) consisting of decrees against us, which was hostile to us; and He has taken it out of the way, having nailed it to the cross.

The word *cheirographon*, which the New American Standard Bible accurately translates as "certificate of debt," means, literally, a handwriting. It is, and always has been, easy for a creditor to claim that they are owed money or for a debtor to claim that they have repaid it. In order to avoid the uncertainty and arguments this could cause, legal systems have always given special emphasis to ways of recording a debt. Until very recently, a common way to commit oneself to make a payment was to sign a check. Handwriting one's signature was the confirmation that one was bound to pay.

In the ancient Greek and Roman world, debts would be recorded in writing, on a wax tablet, papyrus, or vellum. So long as the creditor had the written record of the debt, the debtor was not discharged. Production of the *cheirographon* would be enough to entitle the creditor to seize the debtor and all his possessions to repay the overdue debt.

The debtor would not be free of the debt until the written record had been cancelled. If the certificate of indebtedness was written on a wax tablet, it would have been gently heated and smoothed over so that the record of the debt was erased. If the certificate of indebtedness was written on papyrus, it would have been burned. If it was written on vellum, it would be crossed out. The metaphor we use in English to describe what was happening is this: the debt was *written off*.

The Greek word *exaleipsas* describing the cancellation of our debt of sin is a past tense of the verb *exaleipho*, meaning to plaster over or to wipe out. The word only appears five times in the New Testament. It appears twice in Revelation (Rev 7:17 and Rev 21:4) where on both occasions is refers to God wiping away all tears. The idea of wiping out a debt is closely connected to the Greek word more usually used for forgiveness in the New Testament, *aphiemi*, which literally means "to send away."

The modern version of the hymn "Turn Your Eyes" therefore has it right when it says, in its second verse,

> Turn your eyes to the hillside
> Where justice and mercy embraced
> There the Son of God gave His life for us
> And our measureless debt was erased.

Jesus has taken the debt of sin we have accumulated through our rejection of God's love and our defiance of God's laws and he has obliterated it. Our debts of guilt have been cancelled by our creditor.

How much was the price that Christ paid?

Seventeenth-century theology disappeared down a rabbit hole when theologians got into debates about whether the price paid by Jesus' death was a token payment or whether it was an exact equivalent of the debt incurred by humanity's sin. They forgot that the language about the price being paid is metaphorical but, more importantly, they forgot that the person paying a price was not only a real man, he was also really God. David Bentley Hart is surely correct in reminding us of Anselm's view that Christ's death is a gift of infinite price, a gift exceeding every debt.[28]

To whom was the price paid?

We saw in chapter 1 the difficulties that arise when we think about Jesus' death as a ransom and go on to ask to whom the ransom was paid. The same problem arises in respect of the related metaphor of redemption. The forgiveness metaphor is more helpful than the other two metaphors when thinking about God as the party to whom the price was paid. We belong to God, we owe our lives to God, and we owe a debt of covenant-faithfulness (including our obedience) to God. God is the creditor who must cancel our debts

---

28. Bentley Hart, "A Gift Exceeding Every Debt," 333.

at God's own expense.[29] Just as the redemption metaphor shows us that Jesus paid the price on our behalf, so the forgiveness metaphor shows us that the triune God absorbed into Godself the cost of forgiving our debts.

Friedrich Nietzsche, of all people, grasped this. He understood that the cross was "God's sacrifice of himself for the guilt of human beings, God paying himself back with himself, God as the only one who can redeem man from what for human beings has become impossible to redeem—the creditor sacrifices himself for the debtor."[30]

God was not only the payer but also the payee in the crucial moments which wiped out our indebtedness. As Douglas Webster explains, "The Cross is God Himself in Christ clearing up our moral debts, satisfying what had to be satisfied, what we could never pay, what we could never do."[31] Thinking about our debts of gratitude and guilt as debts owed to God, we then find ourselves at the heart of the mystery of the Trinity. The death of God the Son, as humanity's surety and representative, which discharges those debts, is also the act of God the Father, our creditor, in writing them off.

Conclusion

The metaphors of ransom, redemption, and forgiveness run into one another, like the circles in a Venn diagram. They draw our attention to different aspects of what Jesus did for us through his death and resurrection. The biblical writers are happy to use the metaphors in combination. Ephesians 1:7 declares that in Jesus "we have redemption through his blood, the forgiveness of sins in accordance with the riches of God's grace." The same combination of redemption and forgiveness also appears in Colossians 1:14. The ideas of having our debts bought back, paid off by Jesus and

---

29. Eubank, *Wages of Cross-Bearing*, 154.
30. Nietzsche, *On the Genealogy of Morality*, 292.
31. Webster, *In Debt to Christ*, 54.

Forgiveness and the Debt to God

written off by God the Father, are interchangeable word-pictures for the glorious good news that we no longer carry the burden of a debt we have no hope of repaying ourselves. The question which remains is: How we should live in the light of that startling reality?

The Economy of Resurrection

My words could not tell, not even in part, of the debt of love
that is owed by this thankful heart.

—MATT REDMAN, *I WILL OFFER UP MY LIFE*

WE HAVE SEEN how the ransom metaphor shows us that we are trapped by powers of evil, sin, selfishness, and death. We have looked at how the redemption metaphor reminds us that Jesus was our kinsman-redeemer who paid the cost of rescuing us. We have considered how we are doubly indebted to God, both for every good thing that we have and for every sin that we have committed. What we are now going to think about in this chapter is how those truths should change our lives.

One criticism of the use of imagery from the courtroom to describe the cross (something which appeals to me as a lawyer) is that it risks making what Jesus has done purely external and fails to connect with the difference that believing in Jesus makes in our lives. The same is true of the monetary metaphors. Hans Boersma is not alone in criticizing "the tendency toward a transactional or mercantile understanding of the atonement, in which my sins are transferred or imputed to Christ, while his righteousness is directly transferred or imputed to me."[1] As Steve Holmes puts it, "It is all

1. Boersma, *Violence, Hospitality, and the Cross*, 167.

very well claiming that Jesus has paid the price for my sin, but in what way does that change the way I live in the world?"² The Bible does not leave us to wonder how thinking about the cross in terms of forgiveness, redemption, and ransom should affect the way we live. The New Testament teaches:

1. Because of what God has done for you, be thankful;
2. Because you have been forgiven, forgive your debtors;
3. Because you have been redeemed, live freely;
4. Because you have been ransomed, go to work to set others free (Matt 28).

In this final chapter, I want to highlight what the Bible says about how we are to live as people who know that we have been ransomed, redeemed, and forgiven. We will explore how Jesus' death and resurrection have changed our relationship with God. We will look at Jesus' command that because we have been forgiven we should forgive our debtors. We will consider how our redemption should result in us living freely. We will face up to the challenge that because we have been ransomed, we should work to set others free. But before we look at those points, we need to begin by exploring the truths that our freedom has been certified and that our freedom has done far more than just liberate us from captivity.

Freedom certified

In chapter 2, we discovered the story of Sadeepan, just one of many debt-slaves that IJM has rescued from captivity. Those who brutalize people often brand their victims to mark their ownership or control. When debt-slaves are released, they need proof that they are free, and they need help so that they do not fall back into slavery again. In India, freed debt-slaves such as Sadeepan are issued with official release certificates. The release certificate confirms that the

---

2. Holmes, *The Wondrous Cross*, 72.

holder has been freed and gives them an entitlement to government rehabilitation funds. IJM works with the local government and with the slaves providing aftercare so that former debt-slaves do not find themselves again falling prey to the money-lenders.

In English law, if I owe £100 and the creditor agrees to accept £50 and to write off the balance, the creditor cannot change their mind later and ask me to pay the remainder. But, if I owe £100 and the creditor agrees to write the debt off in full, that agreement is only enforceable if I have written proof of it in a formal document called a "deed." Deeds are documents used to record important transactions, and their contents have to be verified by witnesses. There has to be clear proof that the debt has been forgiven.

Where is our proof that because of Jesus' death, our debt to God has been forgiven? The New Testament gives us multiple proofs. Jesus' resurrection from the dead is proof that God the Father has accepted the payment Jesus has made on our behalf. Our baptism is proof that we participate in Jesus' death and resurrection (Col 2:12). The Holy Spirit is given to us as the *arrabon*, the pledge, deposit, or guarantee, as well as the firstfruit of redemption (Eph 1:13–14; 2 Cor 1:22; Eph 4:30).

In the New Testament, our baptism is the moment our release is certified (Col 3:11–12), our filling with the Holy Spirit is the ongoing assurance of our freedom, and the work of the Spirit within our lives is the continual aftercare our loving heavenly Father provides to prevent us from falling back under the control of the powers of sin, mammon, and death.

As T. F. Torrance stresses, "The church is not simply cleansed by the death of Christ . . . not simply exorcised of unclean spirits, but filled with the Holy Spirit."[3] The death and resurrection of Jesus do far more than release us from captivity and pay off our debts; they guarantee us a future of security, abundance, and purity.

I recently bought a house. The process of house-buying in England is tortuous. Even when you have agreed a price, there are still all sorts of things that can go wrong which mean that the sale falls through. It is only when you have paid a deposit that you are

---

3. Torrance, *Atonement*, 178.

assured that your purchase will go through to completion. The Holy Spirit is the deposit, the down payment, assuring us that we will one day experience a joy far greater than the joy of owning a new home.

Freedom for relationship with God

In both the Old and New Testaments, redemption is intrinsically linked with relationship. In the Old Testament, it is redemption of Israel as God's son, but in the New Testament, it is redemption accomplished by Jesus, the Son of God.

Old Testament: Redemption of God's Son

N. T. Wright is one of a number of theologians who have reminded us of the importance Scripture places on the fact that God treats Israel as his son.[4] Exodus 4 records what God had told Moses to say to Pharaoh. The message, in verse 22, is, "Say to Pharaoh, 'This is what the Lord says: Israel is my firstborn son, and I told you, "Let my son go, so that he may worship me." But you refused to let him go; so I will kill your firstborn son.'"

God here identifies himself as Israel's father and Israel as his firstborn son (and therefore the one entitled to inherit a double portion of the father's wealth). As for the judgment on Egypt, the book of Exodus begins with Pharaoh adopting a genocidal policy of killing all the Israelite baby boys (Exod 1:22). Pharaoh and Egypt will be repaid in their own coin, experiencing some of the horror they had decided to inflict on Israel.

As T. F. Torrance insists, the primary reference of "redemption" is to "*the redemption of Israel out of Egypt as God's firstborn son* which was carried out by God's mighty hand and with the substitutionary sacrifice of the Passover lamb . . . This is a favorite way of speaking of the redemption of Israel in [Deuteronomy]."[5]

---

4. Wright, *The Climax of the* Covenant, 43.
5. Torrance, *Atonement*, 28. Italics original.

Ransomed, Redeemed, and Forgiven

The main image the prophet Hosea uses to describe the relationship between God and Israel is that of a marriage, but in Hosea 11:1–4, he switches to the idea that Israel is God's son:

> When Israel was a child, I loved him,
> and out of Egypt I called my son.
> But the more I called Israel,
> the further they went away from me.
> They sacrificed to the Baals
> and they burned incense to images.
> It was I who taught Ephraim to walk,
> taking them by the arms;
> but they did not realize
> it was I who healed them.
> I led them with cords of human kindness
> with ties of love;
> I lifted the yoke from the neck
> and bent down to feed them.

It isn't difficult for any parent to understand the feelings of God that Hosea is expressing in this passage. God loved Israel and was constantly calling Israel into intimate relationship with him, but the more God called, the more wayward Israel became. Even though God was the one who had taught Israel (referred to as Ephraim, Joseph's son) to walk, who had wiped Israel's bottom, who had treated Israel's grazed knees, who had spoon-fed Israel baby porridge, and who had sought to guide Israel gently, Israel had forgotten all this and rejected a relationship with its loving, heavenly Father.

What God longs for is an intimate relationship with us, a relationship of love and trust and companionship which the Bible describes like the relationship that a bride has to her husband, like the relationship a small boy has to a loving, involved father, like chicks have to the mother hen (Matt 23:37).

New Testament: Redemption by God's Son

In Roman law, the relationship between a master and a slave was expected to continue even after the slave had been freed. The master was still supposed to provide work for the freed slave, while the freed slave was still supposed to honor their patron. But, in exceptional cases, the relationship could go deeper than that. Roman law allowed adults to be adopted (a process called adrogation) but only with the permission of the emperor. The person adopted could then become the heir of their patron.

Paul has this idea of adoption in mind when he is discussing the cross in Galatians 3. Having said in verse 13 that Jesus Christ has redeemed us from the curse of the law, he goes on to say in verse 14 that God " redeemed us in order that the blessing given to Abraham might come to the Gentiles through Christ Jesus, so that by faith we might receive the promise of the Spirit."

The promise given to Abraham was that he would have many children. Those children, Paul argues, were not only the Jews, the natural descendants of Abraham and Sarah, but also those Gentiles who come to faith through Jesus Christ. We have been adopted as children of God the Father because of the work of God the Son. In an utterly unprecedented act, the son of the emperor of the universe has shared his inheritance with us.

Paul makes the same point in Romans 9:4–5: "Theirs [i.e., the Jews'] is *the adoption as sons*; theirs the divine glory, the covenants, the receiving of the law, the temple worship and the promises. Theirs are the patriarchs, and from them is traced the human ancestry of Christ, who is God over all, for ever praised! Amen." Here Paul seamlessly combines the two ways Jesus is God's Son: Jesus is both the eternally-begotten Son of God the Father in his own right, and also, in his humanity, the representative of Israel, God's adopted son.

Galatians 3 confirms that T. F. Torrance is absolutely right that "redemption and inheritance are ... conceptions which in the New Testament cannot be separated out from each other."[6] We are

---

6. Torrance, *Atonement*, 49.

redeemed by our kinsman-redeemer. The only sense in which our redemption is an arms-length transaction is that Jesus stretched out his arms on the cross. We are redeemed because of God's relationship to us, in order that we might enjoy a relationship with God. We are redeemed by Jesus because are his inheritance; as a result we share in Jesus' inheritance from God the Father.

Chapter VIII, article V, of the Westminster Confession of Faith also captures this idea, stating, "The Lord Jesus, by his perfect obedience, and sacrifice of Himself, which He through the eternal Spirit, once offered up unto God, has fully satisfied the justice of his Father; and purchased not only reconciliation, but an everlasting inheritance in the kingdom of heaven, for those whom the Father has given unto Him."[7]

Because of what Jesus has done, we were not only freed from slavery; we were also adopted as heirs of God!

Because you acknowledge your debts to God, you should be thankful

As we saw in the chapter on forgiveness, realizing the extent and nature of our debts to God should inspire us to live lives of thankfulness. We should be constantly thankful for all the good gifts we have from God, both the gifts God has given us as our Creator and the gifts God has given us as our Redeemer.

Living thankful lives is a challenge. We have a natural tendency to take our blessings for granted and to focus on our problems. I remember listening to R. T. Kendall at New Wine in 2017. He told us how, in April 1986, he was in the middle of preaching a sermon at Westminster Chapel on Philippians 4:6 "Don't be anxious about anything but . . . with thanksgiving, let your requests be made known to God," when God convicted him about his own ingratitude. He resolved there and then to live a more thankful life. All too easily we can become grumpy old men or women. My wife and I have introduced into our daily devotional time a thankfulness

---

7. "Westminster Confession of Faith."

journal. Keeping the journal ensures that we begin each day with a focus on the blessings God has given us.

The squeeze toy aliens (a.k.a. the Little Green Men) show us the way to go. In *Toy Story 2*, they say to Mr. Potato Head, "You have saved our lives. We are eternally grateful."[8] How much more should we be eternally grateful for Jesus for what he has done for us? Douglas Webster answers, "To have grasped the message of the cross and to have been forgiven means that every Christian is personally and permanently in Christ's debt. The Christian soul is weighed down no longer by the burden of sin but now by the greater burden of gratitude, a debt which is at one and the same time a possession. As Forsyth put it, 'The great wealth of the church is an exuberant sense that it *owes* everything, and it owes it to Christ.'"[9]

We owe everything to God, but God is not a grasping moneylender. Just as any loving parent would do, God asks that we acknowledge his faithfulness and care by giving token gifts. A good starting point ought to be 10 percent of our income. That's a principle I have tried to live by. It becomes more difficult to tithe the more you have, but that is all the more reason to do it. Wealth is deceitful, constantly seducing us to place our confidence and our security in the wrong places.

Because you have been forgiven, forgive your debtors

In Matthew's Gospel, the consequence of forgiveness is made explicit. Jesus expects those who have been forgiven their debts to go on to forgive their debtors. As we noted in the last chapter, such forgiveness does not mean pretending that the wrongs we have been subjected to do not matter, it does not mean ignoring or excusing the fact that they are wrongs, but it does mean that we do

---

8. Lasseter, *Toy Story 2*.

9. Webster, *In Debt To Christ*, 136, quoting Forsyth, *Missions in State and Church*, 252.

not carry round with us the burden of hatred for those who have hurt us.

The parable of the unmerciful servant

When you forgive, it means you absorb the loss and the debt. You bear it yourself. All forgiveness, then, is costly. That is why Peter, in Matthew 18, asked the obvious question about the extent of our obligation to forgive. How much pain should I absorb, how much cost should I bear, how much forgiveness should I offer? Jesus' answer that we should be prepared to forgive seventy times seven times means that we should be continually prepared to forgive. How is this possible? Only those who know that they have been eternally forgiven can do so.

Jesus then goes on, continuing his answer to Peter's question, to illustrate the size of our debt to God by telling the parable of the ungrateful (or unmerciful) servant. The German theologian Jürgen Moltmann re-tells the parable like this:

> In the parable of the ungrateful servant in Matt. 18:23–35, the kingdom of heaven is "like" a human king who has mercy on his defaulting servant and remits the huge debt he owes. But when this servant refuses to remit the paltry debt of his own debtor, the king has him thrown into prison: "So also my heavenly Father will do to every one of you, if you do not forgive your brother from your heart." The debt remitted by the king (a Jewish metaphor for God) passes all bounds: 100 million dinars. The point of comparison is that our guilt before God is infinitely greater than anything other people owe us; God's mercy with us is infinitely greater than the mercy which God can expect of us. The parable therefore has to do with correspondences between the way God acts and the way human beings act.[10]

The parable of the unmerciful servant hammers home the importance of our obligation to forgive others. The image is simple

---

10. Moltmann, *Experiences in Theology*, 164.

enough to grasp. There is a man who owes the king an unpayable debt. The size of the debt is astronomical; not even a lottery win would be enough to pay it off. According to the figures of the ancient historian Josephus, the debt the unmerciful servant owed the king was forty times the amount of tax Judaea paid to Rome annually. The king graciously forgives the man. The man's next move is to go and find a fellow servant who owes him a far smaller amount of money, and to force him to pay up. Such an action so offends the king that he rescinds his own offer of forgiveness.

The Lord's Prayer

The same message is to be found, in equally stark terms, in the Lord's Prayer itself. In Matthew 6:12 Jesus taught his followers to pray, "Forgive us our debts, as we also have forgiven our debtors." The Lord's Prayer is a prayer for debt-cancellation, immediately followed by the warning. Nathan Eubank suggests translating Matthew 6:12 as "Cancel our debts for us, as we too cancel for those in debt to us."[11]

The message of the parable of the unmerciful servant and of Jesus' own commentary on the Lord's Prayer is that "Those who do not imitate God's willingness to cancel the debts of others will not have their debts cancelled (Matt 18:23–35)."[12] God will repay us in our own coin: if we forgive others the debts they owe us, God will forgive us the unpayable debt we owe him; if we refuse to forgive others, God will withhold God's forgiveness from us.

Interest-free loans and gift-loans

Because Christians have been forgiven, we should forgive others. Moreover, the economy of resurrection encourages us to make gift-loans. Lending in a family context can be a recipe for enormous blessing or it can be a recipe for disaster. I once did a case in which

---

11. Eubank, *Wages of Cross-Bearing*, 54.
12. Eubank, *Wages of Cross-Bearing*, 204.

a lady in her nineties had been tricked out of her life savings by her nephew, who had demanded that he repay a loan of £5,000 he had made to her son, even though the nephew had already made the son bankrupt over the same debt. The nephew's unwillingness to forgive the small debt his cousin owed him destroyed the family. For this reason, Ted Rossman, an analyst at CreditCards.com, recommends that, when lending to your family, "Don't lend more than you can afford to lose. Ideally, I think those arrangements are best treated as gifts."[13]

We should be prepared to lend to our family, to our fellow believers, and to the poor without charging interest but, more than that, we should be prepared to treat such loans as gifts. In Luke 6:33–36, Jesus taught,

> If you do good to those who are good to you, what credit is that to you? Even sinners do that. And if you lend to those from whom you expect repayment, what credit is that to you? Even sinners lend to sinners, expecting to be repaid in full. But love your enemies, do good to them, and lend to them without expecting to get anything back. Then your reward will be great, and you will be children of the Most High, because he is kind to the ungrateful and wicked. Be merciful, just as your Father is merciful.

In lending without expecting to receive anything in return, Jesus' followers show themselves to be God's children.

In the US, the Medical Debt Relief Alliance goes one stage further. In a country where medical debt is a contributing cause in 66 percent of all bankruptcies, the Medical Debt Relief Alliance buys up unpayable medical debt from creditors and then cancels it. In so doing, they are reflecting the example of Jesus, who P. T. Forsyth described as having bought up all other debts through his death on the cross.[14]

---

13. Horch, "Loaning Money to Friends and Family?"
14. Forsyth, *The Work of Christ*, 156.

Because you have been redeemed, live freely

Being redeemed means being set free from slavery. As ones who have been freed from slavery, we should live freely; we should live in ways which do not lead to others being enslaved, and we should work to free others from slavery.

Living freely

Alastair Roberts and Andrew Wilson write, "We were slaves to sin, death, fear, the flesh, and the Devil. But at just the right time, God rescued us. He defeated our enemy and redeemed us through the blood of his Son, taking us through the waters of baptism, uniting us to himself, giving us his Spirit to lead us and guide us, and providing us with all we need. He did all this not so that we could do our own thing, but so that we could do his thing."[15]

Because we have been bought by Christ we ought not willingly to become slaves of anyone or anything else. In 1 Corinthians 7:21–23, Paul reassures those who are slaves that Christ has given them the freedom that ultimately matters, but he goes on to advise them to take advantage of any opportunity they may have to become free. Conversely, Paul tells those who are free not to become slaves of any human masters. In the ancient world, this would have required a certain amount of self-restraint and careful management of the household finances.

Just as Paul urges the Corinthian church in 1 Corinthians 7 not to become slaves to any human masters, so he also reminds them in 1 Corinthians 6:19 that because they have been bought with a price they ought to glorify God with the use they make of their bodies. He warns them against falling back into the kinds of slavery from which they have been released, whether legalism, addiction, or immorality.

For Christians, living freely is living faithfully. The Ten Commandments are introduced in the book of Exodus with the words "I am the Lord your God, who brought you out of Egypt, out of

---

15. Roberts and Wilson, *Echoes of Exodus*, 142.

the land of slavery" (Exod 20:2). God's law is given to the people God loves.

The Ten Commandments are part of God's covenant with the people of Israel. A covenant *(berit)* is a relationship of faithfulness and mutual loyalty. The term is used to describe both the relationship between a powerful country and its vassal state and to describe the relationship between marriage partners.

Because God is God and we are not, an essential fact of our relationship with God is that we are called to obey God, to acknowledge that God really does know best for our lives. We are called to trust God's commands like a well-trained dog responds to its owner's voice or like a child who has learned from wise, consistent discipline that what Mommy says really is best.

But because God is love, the most essential fact of our relationship with God is that God loves us with a love that will never give up on us, and we are called to love God back with all our heart, soul, mind, and strength. It is safe to admit our dependence on God, and wise to obey God's commands, because we are loved by God; loved with a love deeper and more secure than that which the most devoted husband has ever loved his wife.

However, if our understanding of living faithfully is limited to thinking in terms of living in accordance with God's laws, we risk living like the resentful brother in the parable of the prodigal son. Christians are not merely bond-servants who are obliged to obey God. Christians are children of God who should long to show their love to their wonderful heavenly Father.

The reason the Bible returns, again and again, to the idea that the relationship between God and God's people or between Christ and his church is like the relationship between a husband and wife is because that metaphor puts God's laws into their proper context. In my marriage to my wife there have been some moments when I have felt the challenge of the command "Do not commit adultery," but my sexual faithfulness to my wife is the least she deserves. Covenant-faithfulness to my wife involves far more than not actually sleeping with anyone else, and much more than simply not thinking about sleeping with anyone else.

Ephesians 5:28 says that husbands owe a debt to love their wives as they love their own bodies. The Greek verb used here is *opheiló*, the same verb used in the Lord's Prayer (Matt 6:12; Luke 11:4) and which Paul uses when talking about our continuing *debt* to love one another (Rom 13:8).

The debt of love I owe to my wife involves contributing what I can to the household finances, spending time with my wife, being interested in her and her activities, showing her respect and care and attention in all the small, personalized ways which enrich and bless her. I don't often have to check consciously whether I am obeying my marriage vows; my focus is more on the wonderful person I am married to than it is on the rules our relationship and the promises I have made commit me to following.

In the same way, Paul writes in 2 Corinthians 5:14–15, "Christ's love compels us, because we are convinced that one died for all, and therefore all died. And he died for all, that those who live should no longer live for themselves but for him who died for them and was raised again." Because Jesus has died for us, we should not live for ourselves but for him. Our eagerness to obey God should be a demonstration of our love for God's Son rather than an end in itself.

I travel frequently to Albania. The local currency there is the *lek*. If I return to England and try to buy anything using my *lek*, the payment I offer will be refused because I am trying to pay in the wrong currency. The teaching of Jesus and the apostles is that human beings are always trying to pay God in the wrong currency. We try to please God through our works, through our efforts to make our behavior match up with what we think God requires of us. Often the impression we are given is that our works are not enough; that the repayment we are offering is too small, that if only we did more good works we would be able to raise our credit with God sufficient to be able to pay off our debt.

The writer to the Hebrews makes it clear that so long as we are depending on our works to repay our debt to God, we are trying to pay God in the wrong currency. "Without faith it is impossible to please God" (Heb 11:6). The currency which God accepts is faith, not good works. Good works are how we demonstrate our relationship with God, not how we make it.

Live according to the family likeness

One of the things that happens as you get older is that you discover yourself looking and acting more like your parents. As children of God, Christians are supposed to display the family likeness and to be involved in the family business.

The images to do with money that the Bible links to our redemption do not focus on the cross in isolation. The price was paid on the cross, the resurrection demonstrates that the payment was effective to secure our release, and the giving of the Holy Spirit is the deposit which seals our freedom and the working capital which resources us to act justly. The Holy Spirit is also the one who confirms our adoption as the children of God the Father.

As children of God, we are supposed to show a family likeness. The term the Bible uses to describe the family likeness we are supposed to display is "holiness." P. T. Forsyth reminds us that "you cannot talk about Christ and his death in any thorough way without talking about the holiness of God."[16] Jesus' sacrifice was only acceptable to God because Jesus had lived a holy life. Jesus died not only to free us from the crushing weight of our failure to live lives worthy of God, Jesus also died in order to unleash the power of the Holy Spirit so that we would be enable to live more justly and purely.

P. T. Forsyth insisted that God is Holy Love. We are given God's laws in order that we might understand what Love is like. God's laws show us, as 1 Corinthians 13 and the fruit of Spirit also show us, that God calls us to the same Holy Love. We are called to respond to God's loving-kindness *(hesed)* towards us by demonstrating the same covenant-faithfulness towards God and towards those we are brought into relationship with.

---

16. Forsyth, *The Work of Christ*, 45.

How can we, as adopted children, display the family likeness? The answer the New Testament gives is because of the Holy Spirit. The Holy Spirit is not only the down payment on our inheritance; he is also the motive power enabling us to remain free. The great fourth-century preacher John Chrysostom said in his *Homilies on Romans 13:* "Christ not only set us free without demanding any payment for his services; he also equipped us for greater struggles in the future."[17]

The apostle Paul makes this clear in the opening verses of Romans 8 (when he introduces the Holy Spirit into his argument for the first time in the letter). Jesus Christ's death has freed us from condemnation (verse 1) and the law of the Spirit of life has freed us from the law of sin and death (verse 2) in order that we might live according to the Holy Spirit and so demonstrate the justice which God's laws demanded (verse 4).

The Holy One of Israel who redeemed us did so in order that we might reflect God's own holiness in our lives. Jesus Christ "is not only the pledge to us of God's love, but the pledge to God of our sure response to it in a total change of will and life."[18]

Titus 2:13–14 expressly links our redemption with our purification. We are redeemed from our lawless deeds (our selfish acts of disobedience to God's laws) and we are reoriented by the Holy Spirit so that we become zealous for good deeds. Our God and Savior Jesus Christ gave himself for us so that he might purify for himself a people for his own possession.

Living in ways that do not lead to others being enslaved

Paul, in Romans 13, says this:

> Let no debt remain outstanding, except the continuing debt to love one another, for he who loves his fellow man has fulfilled the law. The commandments, "Do not commit adultery," "Do not murder," "Do not steal," "Do not

---

17. Chrysostom, "Homily 13 on Romans."
18. Forsyth, *The Work of Christ*, 195.

covet," and whatever other commandment there may be, are summed up in this one rule: "Love your neighbor as yourself." Love does no harm to its neighbor. Therefore love is the fulfillment of the law.

What Paul is saying is the same thing Jesus said repeatedly in the Gospels. God's law, expressed in the Ten Commandments and elsewhere in Scripture, is really an explanation of the two Great Commandments, "Love the Lord your God with all your heart, soul, mind, and strength" and "Love your neighbor as yourself." Love is not all about law, but God's laws are all about love.

It is easy for us to become comfortable Christians, confident in our self-righteousness and ignorant of our impact on others. We increasingly live in a world in which our choices have a ripple effect on those who we may never meet. The plastic packaging my food comes in pollutes the ocean, causing further harm to fish. The fast fashion I buy is produced by workers in Bangladesh and Vietnam on starvation wages. The airplane I take to go on holiday contributes to global warming against which I can protect myself but the poorest can not.

Living freely and loving our neighbors demands that we do more than simply not acting maliciously. Loving our neighbors means being concerned for them, actively considering their interests in all the choices we make. For those neighbors we know, the practices of sharing, of generosity, and of interest-free lending are all ways in which we can help prevent those who suffer temporary calamity from being permanently oppressed. For those we don't know, it is about lifestyle choices which put others first, it is about active resistance to the kingdom of comfort which encourages us to think only about ourselves and our circle. My good friend Peter Grant suggests some practical things we can do which could make a big difference in his book *Poor No More: Be Part of a Miracle—Nine Ways in Which You Can Have an Impact on Global Poverty.*

The Economy of Resurrection

Because you have been ransomed, go to work to set others free

Ananias's story

In 2012, I travelled to Uganda to see firsthand the legal aid work of the Ugandan Christian Lawyers Fraternity (UCLF). In a country where lawyers are unaffordable for the vast majority of the population, the UCLF provides free legal assistance in police stations and prisons. Its presence alone reduces the incidence of abuse and mistreatment.

One of the people I met was Ananias. Many years earlier, he had been a law student. He was arrested by the police one night on his way home. A serious crime had been committed, and because the most likely suspect had political connections, the police were looking for someone else to blame. Ananias was put into prison on remand, where he remained for several years. Long periods of imprisonment before trial are commonplace but because the paperwork relating Ananias's case was lost, officially he did not exist anymore. When a paralegal working for the UCLF met him in prison, the UCLF were able to put together a dossier, get Ananias's case before a court, and get him released because of the total lack of evidence against him.

When I met Ananias, he was working as a paralegal for the UCLF, going back into police stations and prisons, providing legal advice to others in similar situations to the one he had experienced himself. Ananias, who had been ransomed himself, was now working to set others free. Nine years after I met him, Ananias now leads the work of the UCLF's paralegals.

What does it mean to live as people who know that we have been ransomed from the power of evil? How do we live a life which, in all its aspects, pleases God? In order to answer those questions we need to understand the relationship of the two Great Commandments to each other and to the Great Commission.

How the first and second Great Commandments fit together

Jesus draws out the heart of the law of Moses. It hangs, he says, on two Great Commandments. The Greatest Commandment is to love the Lord your God with all your heart, with all your soul, with all your mind, and with all your strength (Matt 22:37–38). But Jesus immediately adds that the second Great Commandment is like it (Matt 22:39). How is the command to love your neighbor as yourself like the command to love God?

The answer the Bible gives is that the love we show to our neighbors is our demonstration of our love for God. It is impossible to love God without expressing that love in love for our neighbors. The way that God wants us to acknowledge our debt of gratitude for God, our love for God, is by paying it forward through our love for others. This is clear throughout the Bible but the point is made especially clearly by what the Old Testament says about Josiah.

Josiah became king when he was just eight years old and he reigned for thirty-one years. He is praised in 2 Kings 22:2 because "He did what was right in the eyes of the Lord." He undertook a program of repairs to the temple (2 Kgs 22:5), he led the people in a national renewal of their commitment to God (2 Kgs 23:3), conducted major reforms to the worship of God, and organized one of the biggest Passover celebrations ever seen (2 Chr 35:18). He was a great religious reformer, a man whose zeal for God was almost unparalleled.

2 Kings 23:25 gives Josiah the highest praise. It says, "Neither before nor after Josiah was there a king like him who turned to the Lord as he did—with all his heart and with all his soul and with all his strength, in accordance with all the law of Moses." Josiah is clearly commended as a man who was wholehearted for God, who tried his hardest to fulfill the first Great Commandment. The effect of Josiah's reign was remarkable. 2 Chronicles 34:33 tells us that "As long as he lived, the people did not fail to follow the Lord, the God of their fathers."

Jeremiah compared the sons of Josiah, Shallum (Jehoahaz) and Jehoiakim, with their father.

> "Woe to him who builds his palace by unrighteousness, his upper rooms by injustice, making his countrymen work for nothing, not paying them for their labor... Does it make you a king to have more and more cedar? Did not your father have food and drink?
> He did what was right and just, so all went well with him. He defended the cause of the poor and needy, and so all went well. Is that not what it means to know me?" declares the Lord. "But your eyes and your heart are set only on dishonest gain, on shedding innocent blood and on oppression and extortion." (Jer 22:13–17)

God's words, spoken through Jeremiah, should shock us. God is saying that the two Great Commandments are so closely connected that those who truly love God will inevitably express that love for God in their actions to defend the poor and the needy, the marginalized, the disadvantaged, the friendless, and the outcast.

The commandment to love God cannot be fulfilled without also fulfilling the command to love our neighbors. The letter of 1 John makes the same point in the New Testament. 1 John 4:20 points out, "Whoever claims to love God yet hates a brother or sister is a liar. For whoever does not love their brother and sister, whom they have seen, cannot love God, whom they have not seen."

How the Great Commandments and the Great Commission fit together

At the end of Matthew 28, Jesus gave his disciples the Great Commission. We usually remember it as him saying to them, "Go into all the world and make disciples of all nations." How does the Great Commission relate to the two Great Commandments?

The Great Commission and the two Great Commandments are not to be opposed to one another. They are not mutually exclusive and we do not have to choose between them. On the contrary, you cannot fulfill the Great Commission without obeying the two Great Commandments, nor can you obey the two Great Commandments without being committed to the fulfillment of the Great Commission.

What Jesus actually told his disciples in Matthew 28 was to "make disciples of all nations, *teaching them to obey everything I have commanded you*," and the things which Jesus commanded us to do were to love God with all our heart, soul, mind, and strength and to love our neighbors as ourselves (Matt 22:37–40). So the fulfillment of the Great Commission necessarily involves teaching people how to love God and to love their neighbors. If we do not do that, we have not, however high a priority we place on evangelism, fulfilled the Great Commission.

Conversely, if we love our neighbors as ourselves, then we will want our neighbors to know God and to be assured of eternal life in God's presence and so our love for them will inevitably lead us to take the opportunities which present themselves to tell them about Jesus. Moreover, our witness to Christ will be all the more effective if we have truly shown love for our neighbors in other, more practical ways.

Paying forward, not paying back

Our indebtedness to God, to our family, and to society for the fact of our existence, our talents, and the opportunities to develop and exercise them, and for the conditions in which we live and may prosper, is different in its nature to our indebtedness because of the evil and violence which we have thought, said, and done.

Sin incurs a debt which has to be paid back. The condemnation and punishment it merits is retributive. Retribution seeks to measure the guilt and harm caused by an evil act, and to quantify the maximum penalty which could be imposed. The establishment of that maximum then forms the yardstick against which commutation, compounding, and compromise of the penalty may take place.

Our original indebtedness is a debt which is not to be paid back but to be paid forward. The economics of paying back is a zero-sum game; the economics of paying forward is a positive-sum game. Zero-sum games are games in which one side wins and another loses. Positive-sum games are games in which everyone wins.

The death of Christ transforms the logic of debts of guilt, replacing it with the logic of debts of gratitude. Debts of gratitude are not so much paid back as paid forward. That is what Jesus calls us also to do with debts of guilt. Paying forward a debt breaks the economics of payback.

As a penniless young man studying in France I was shown enormous kindness by Clive and Christine Charlton, a couple pastoring the Eglise Evangélique Libre in Toulouse. They gave me hospitality, inviting me to join them for meals and providing accommodation for my fiancée which I could not afford. When I asked how I could repay them, they answered that rivers do more good than lakes. The way to acknowledge my debt to them was not to seek to do them good, but to do good to others when I had the opportunity.

I was taught the same lesson when walking as a teenager from a campsite in Cornwall to the nearest town. Someone driving a car stopped and offered me a lift. When I asked how I could thank him, he said remember what I have done and be prepared to do the same for someone else in future.

When I was younger, my brother got himself into debt. Although he was working, he could not make ends meet. He asked me for help. When I looked at his income and outgoings I could see that although he had enough to pay his bills, he could not afford to repay the debt he had accumulated. I gave him an interest-free loan to pay off that debt and to stabilize his finances so that he could move forward.

In making that interest-free loan to my brother, I remembered how I had been able to study at university because of an interest-free loan made to me by one of my great-uncles. I honored my great-uncle's generosity to me not only by paying him back but also by copying his action, paying it forward to my brother.

Interest-free loans have the power to transform people's financial situations. They enable the recipients to avoid financial catastrophe when income temporarily dries up or when their financial wellbeing is threatened by a unexpected expense. Christians disagree about the extent to which the charging of interest is immoral, but at the very least we ought to practice making interest-free loans to our families (1 Tim 6:8), to our fellow believers (Deut 23:19; Neh 5:10), and to the poor (Exod 22:25; Lev 25:36–37; Ps 15:5; Prov 28:8; Ezek 18:8).

I pay forward the debt I owe to the Charltons whenever I open my house and my table to those not in a position to compensate me. I do not measure how often I do this by the number of times I was fed and hosted by the Charltons; I do this whenever I have opportunity. In the same way, I pay forward the debt I owe to the man who gave me a lift whenever I have opportunity to do likewise. The economics of paying forward is not the economics of addition and subtraction; it is the economics of multiplication and the removal of division.

The atonement is the crux of the conflict between the economics of paying back and the economics of paying forward. To ask how the death of the God-man Jesus Christ could be the equivalent of the penalty which the whole of sinful humanity needed to pay back to God is to pose the question in the terms of the old economics.

The equation of which Christ's death and resurrection are the crux does not balance. Instead of the equals sign (=), there is the greater-than (>) sign. The New Testament resonates with the words *how much more*. If we want to give good gifts to our children, how much more does God the Father want to give us the Holy Spirit (Luke 11:13)? If we have been justified by Jesus' blood, how much more will we saved from God's wrath through him (Rom 5:9)? If we have been reconciled to God the Father through the death of Jesus, how much more, having been reconciled, shall we be saved through Jesus' resurrected life (Rom 5:10)? If Adam's disobedience led to the reign of death over the human race, how much more did Jesus' obedience lead to overflowing blessings, including eternal life, for many (Rom 5:15–17)? How much more glorious is the justice which Jesus brings than the law of Moses, which could only condemn (2 Cor 3:9)?

How much more is the death of God's own Son worth than the wages of human sinfulness? How much more has the resurrection achieved than simply the removal of the curse of death? How much more does the giving of the Holy Spirit promise than simply the power to obey God's law? The new life guaranteed by the resurrection of Jesus Christ is so much more than the continuation of human life on its existing terms minus the curses of sin and death. It is adoption into the family of God.

Even our earthly families are communities in which the iron laws of economics do not apply. In our world, the family or household unit is the unit where exchange occurs without money, where the cost of serving others is not counted, and where forgiveness is shown and received.

In the community of the resurrection, gift and mutuality displace any calculations of self-interest or the hoarding of scarce resources. God's extravagant blessings on those who, however faithful they have tried to be, will forever be in God's debt are a multiple of the blessings lavished by a billionaire father.

God, who does not stand in need of anything from us, wants us to pay forward our debt to him by acting lovingly, justly, and mercifully toward one another. Irenaeus quotes Proverbs 19:17, which says, "He that gives alms to the poor loans to the Lord."[19] In the same way, in Matthew 25:31–46, followers of Jesus are to pay forward our debt to him by feeding the hungry, giving the thirsty something to drink, housing the homeless, clothing the naked, and visiting the sick and those in prison.

Jesus encourages his followers not to lay up treasure for themselves on earth, but with their heavenly Father (Matt 5:43–48). Only investments in heaven are safe from the moths, robbers, stock market collapses, recessions, pandemics, and other dangers which make investments on earth so risky. Only investments in heaven are truly perpetual. As Nathan Eubank says, "Tremendous

---

19. Irenaeus, *Against Heresies*, IV.18.6.

faith in God's reliability is an unspoken assumption in the Sermon [on the Mount] as a whole; one must 'wager' one's life on the belief that God can and will repay what God has promised."[20]

The risk of choosing to build up an investment in heaven rather than focusing on investments on earth is, Jesus says, no risk at all. Our investment in heaven comes backed by a deposit guarantee infinitely more reliable than that offered by the US Federal Deposit Insurance Corporation or the UK Financial Services Compensation Scheme. Even if all our investments on earth were to pay off to the point that we became ruler of the whole world, they would still be worthless if our own life was forfeit (Matt 16:24–26).

God's promises are outrageous in terms of human economics. Those who have given up earthly possessions and family connections (Matt 19:29) are promised that they will be repaid a hundred times as much. In my experience as a banking lawyer, any offer of more than 10 percent interest is too good to be true and the sign of a scam. Yet Jesus tells us that God outdoes Bernard Madoff, Allen Stanford, Charles Ponzi, and all the other conmen in terms of the promises he makes to those who will sell everything they own in order to buy into him.

God owes us nothing, and yet the New Testament proclaims that God will reward us far beyond anything we deserve.

Conclusion

There is nothing economical about the cross and resurrection. Jesus did not do *just enough* to ransom us from the power of evil and to pay off the debt to God. Jesus paid an incalculable cost and was rewarded by God the Father for doing so with us as his inheritance (Eph 1:18). Jesus' death and resurrection and the giving of the Holy Spirit are all extravagant, excessive, awesome demonstrations of the depths of God's love and faithfulness.

Anselm knew this truth, saying, "He freed us from our sins, and from his own wrath, and from hell, and from the power of the

---

20. Eubank, *Wages of Cross-Bearing*, 85.

devil, whom he came to vanquish for us, because we are unable to do it, and he purchased for us the kingdom of heaven; and by doing all these things, he manifested the greatness of his love toward us."[21]

The word-pictures to do with money that the Bible uses to help us to see a small part of what Jesus' death and resurrection mean are not supposed to be cold transactional metaphors. They are meant to change us.

Because of the enormity of the debts to God for which we have been forgiven, we are given the resources to be able to unleash the power of forgiveness to those who have hurt us. Because our redemption by our kinsman-redeemer means our adoption as children of God and is sealed with the gift of the Holy Spirit, we are given the strength we need to be able to live free, holy, and pure lives. Because we know what it is to be ransomed from the power of evil, we have been freed from fear and empowered to be able to work to set others free.

Jesus' death and resurrection have equipped Christians with the resources to forgive our debtors, to pursue holiness, and to join with God in God's work of setting others free, because God's presence and power have been poured out on us when the Holy Spirit was released at Pentecost.

Our debts of guilt have been written off. Forgiveness replaces the death-dealing logic of payback with the life-giving logic of paying forwards. In the world to come, the only debts we will carry are the debts of gratitude. There will be two debts that will be rolled over forever, which, as a matter of principle, will never have to be repaid: the debt of love we owe to God who lavishes gifts on us beyond our imagining, and the debt of love we owe to one another.

---

21. Anselm, *Cur Deus Homo?* 1.5.

Bibliography

Anderson, Gary A. *Sin: A History*. New Haven, CT: Yale University Press, 2009.
Anonymous. "Incomplete Work on Matthew, Homily 4." In *Ancient Christian Devotional: A Year of Weekly Readings*, edited by Cindy Crosby, 46. Downers Grove, IL: InterVarsity, 2007.
———. "Old Gallican Missal." In *Ancient Christian Devotional: A Year of Weekly Readings*, edited by Cindy Crosby, 105. Downers Grove, IL: InterVarsity, 2007.
Anselm. *Cur Deus Homo?* In *Anselm of Canterbury: The Major Works*, edited by Brian Davies and G. R. Evans, 260–356. Oxford: Oxford University Press, 1998.
Augustine. *De diversis questionibus ad Simplicianum*. In *The Works of Saint Augustine: A Translation for the 21st Century*, edited by B. Ramsey, translated by R. Canning, 7:171–210. Hyde Park, NY: New City, 2008.
———. *On The Trinity*. Translated by E. Hill. Brooklyn, NY: New City Press, 1991.
Bell, Daniel M. "Only Jesus Saves: Towards a Theopolitical Ontology of Judgement." In *Theology and the Political: The New Debate*, edited by C. Davis et al., 200–230. London: Duke University Press, 2005.
Bentley Hart, David. *The Beauty of the Infinite: The Aesthetics of Christian Truth*. Grand Rapids, MI: Eerdmans, 2003.
———. "A Gift Exceeding Every Debt: An Eastern Orthodox Appreciation of Anselm's *Cur Deus Homo*." *Pro Ecclesia* 7 (1998) 333–49.
Benveniste, Emile. *Le Vocabulaire des Institutions Indo-Européennes*. Paris: Minuit, 1969.
Berman, Harold J. *Law and Revolution: The Foundation of the Western Legal Tradition*. Cambridge, UK: Cambridge University Press, 1983.
Bicknell E. J. *A Theological Introduction to the Thirty-Nine Articles of the Church of England*. 2nd ed. London: Longmans, Green & Co., 1942.
Bieler, André. *Calvin's Economic and Social Theory*. Translated by J. Greig. Geneva: World Alliance of Reformed Churches, 2005.
Blenkinsopp, Joseph. *Isaiah 40–55: A New Translation with Introduction and Commentary*. New York: Doubleday, 2002.
Boersma, Hans. *Heavenly Participation: The Weaving of a Sacramental Tapestry*. Grand Rapids, MI: Eerdmans, 2011.

BIBLIOGRAPHY

———. *Violence, Hospitality and the Cross: Reappropriating the Atonement Tradition*. Grand Rapids, MI: Eerdmans, 2004.
Bomberger, E. Douglas, ed. *Brainard's Biographies of American Musicians*. Westport, CT: Greenwood, 1999.
Burke, Edmund. *Reflections on the Revolution in France*. 1790. Reprint, London: Penguin, 1986.
Calvin, John. *Commentary on 1 Timothy*. In *Calvin's Commentaries: The Second Epistle of Paul the Apostle to the Corinthians and the Epistles to Timothy, Titus and Philemon*, translated by T. A. Smail, 184–285. Edinburgh: The Saint Andrew Press, 1964. https://www.ccel.org/ccel/calvin/calcom43.iii.iv.i.html.
Carey, George. "Chains around Africa: Crisis or Hope for the New Millennium?" In *Proclaim Liberty: Reflections on Theology and Debt*, edited by Susan Hawley, 15–24. London: Christian Aid, 1998.
Chafe, Perry, Allan Hawco, and Malcolm MacRury, dir. *Republic of Doyle*. Toronto, Canada: Canadian Broadcasting Corporation, 2014.
Chandler, Paul, and Rachel Chandler. *Hostage: A Year at Gunpoint with Somali Gangsters*. Chicago: Chicago Review, 2011.
Chrysostom, John. *Homilies of St. John Chrysostom on the Epistle of St. Paul to the Romans*. Scotts Valley, CA: CreateSpace, 2012.
———. "Homily 13 on Romans." In *Ancient Christian Devotional: A Year of Weekly Readings*, edited by Cindy Crosby, 163. Downers Grove, IL: InterVarsity, 2007.
Cowan, David. *Economic Parables: The Monetary Teachings of Jesus Christ*. Milton Keynes, UK: Paternoster, 2006.
Derrida, Jacques. *On Cosmopolitanism and Forgiveness*. Abingdon, UK: Routledge, 2001.
Dickens, Charles. *David Copperfield*. 1850. Reprint, London: Hazell, Watson & Viney, 1935.
———. *Little Dorrit*. 1856. Reprint, London: Hazell, Watson & Viney, 1935.
———. *The Pickwick Papers*. 1868. Reprint, London: Hazell, Watson & Viney, 1935.
Dodaro, Robert, and George Lawless, eds. *Augustine and His Critics: Essays in Honour of Gerald Bonner*. London: Routledge, 2002.
Dudley-Smith, Timothy. "Lord, for the Years." Carol Stream, IL: Hope Publishing, 1969.
Edwards, Jonathan. "Discourse on Justification." In *The Works of Jonathan Edwards, Volume One*, edited by Henry Rogers, 622–54. New York: Daniel Appleton and Co., 1835.
Eubank, Nathan. *Wages of Cross-Bearing and Debt of Sin: The Economy of Heaven in Matthew's Gospel*. Beihefte Zeitschrift für die Neutestamentliche Wissenscharft 196. Berlin: De Gruyter, 2013.
Evans, G. R. *Law and Theology in the Middle Ages*. London: Routledge, 2002.
Founds, Rick. "Lord I Lift Your Name on High." Brentwood, TN: Brentwood Benson Publishing, 1989.
Forsyth, P. T. *The Justification of God: Lectures for War-Time on a Christian Theodicy*. London: Latimer House, 1948.

Bibliography

———. *Missions in State and Church: Sermons and Addresses*. 1908. Reprint, Amsterdam: Leopold Classic Library, 2018.
———. *The Work of Christ*. 2nd ed. London: Independent Press, 1938.
Getty, Keith, and Stuart Townsend. "In Christ Alone." Eastbourne, UK: ThankYou Music, 2001.
Johnston, Julia H. "He Ransomed Me." 1916.
Girard, René. *I See Satan Fall Like Lightning*. Translated by James G. Williams. Maryknoll, NY: Orbis, 2001.
Giraud, Cédric, and Constant J. Mews, eds. *Liber Pancrisis, un Florilège des Pères et des Maîtres Modernes du XIIe Siècle*. Brussels: Union Académique Internationale, 2006.
Graeber, David. *Debt: The First 5,000 Years*. London: Melville, 2014.
Grant, Peter. *Poor No More: Be Part of a Miracle—Nine Ways in Which You Can Have an Impact on Global Poverty*. Oxford: Monarch, 2008.
Gregory of Nazianus. "Dogmatic Poems." In *Ancient Christian Doctrine 3: We Believe in the Crucified and Risen Lord*, edited by Mark J. Edwards, 124. Madison, WI: IVP Academic, 2009.
———. *Oration 45*. In *Nicene and Post-Nicene Fathers, Second Series*, edited by Philip Schaff and Henry Wace, 7:422–34. 1894. Reprint, Peabody, MA: Hendrickson, 1994.
Gregory of Nyssa. *The Great Catechism*. In *Nicene and Post-Nicene Fathers, Second Series*, edited by Philip Schaff and Henry Wace, translated by William Moore and Henry Austin Wilson, 5:492–93. 1892. Reprint, Peabody, MA: Hendrickson, 1994.
Gunton, Colin E. *The Actuality of Atonement: A Study of Metaphor, Rationality and the Christian Tradition*. London: T. & T. Clark, 1988.
Hays, Richard B. *First Corinthians: Interpretation: A Bible Commentary for Teaching and Preaching*. Louisville, KY: Westminster John Knox, 2011.
"Heidelberg Catechism." https://www.ccel.org/creeds/heidelberg-cat.html.
Holmes, Stephen R. *The Wondrous Cross: Atonement and Penal Substitution in the Bible and History*. Milton Keynes, UK: Paternoster, 2007.
Horch, A. J. "Loaning Money to Friends and Family? Treat It as a Gift and Not a Loan." *CNBC* July 5, 2020. https://www.cnbc.com/2020/07/05/loaning-money-to-friends-and-family-treat-it-as-a-gift-and-not-a-loan.html.
Horner, Robert. "The Beatitudes for Lawyers." Lecture, Lawyers' Christian Fellowship, October 5, 2020.
Hudson, Michael. . . . *And Forgive Them Their Debts: Lending, Foreclosure, and Redemption from Bronze Age Finance to the Jubilee Year*. Forest Hills, NY: Institute for the Study of Long-term Economic Trends, 2018.
Huxley, Aldous. *Brave New World*. London: Chatto & Windus, 1932.
Irenaeus of Lyons. *Against Heresies*. In *The Ante-Nicene Fathers*, edited by Alexander Roberts and James Donaldson, 309–567. New York: Scribner's, 1899.
Johnston, Philip. *Deuteronomy: The People's Bible Commentary*. Oxford: Bible Reading Fellowship, 2005.
Kadaré, Ismail. *Broken April*. Translated by John Hodgson. London: Saqi Books, 1990.

BIBLIOGRAPHY

Kardol, Kate. "Five Interesting Facts You Need to Know about Modern Slavery and Exploitation." *Tearfund* July 29, 2020. https://www.tearfund.org.nz/The-Tearfund-Blog-(1)/July-2020/Five-interesting-facts-about-modern-slavery.aspx.

Kendrick, Graham. "Amazing Love (My Lord What Love Is This)." Tunbridge Wells, UK: Make Way Music, 1989.

Kirkby, John. *Nevertheless: The Incredible Story of One Man's Mission to Change Thousands of People's Lives*. 5th ed. Bradford, UK: Christians Against Poverty, 2010.

Lasseter, John, dir. *Toy Story 2*. Emeryville, CA: Pixar Animation Company, 1999.

Lees Bancroft, Charitie. "Before the Throne of God Above." 1867.

Lewis, C. S. *The Last Battle*. 1956. Reprint, London: William Collins, 1980.

———. *The Lion, The Witch and the Wardrobe*. London: Geoffrey Bles, 1950.

———. *Mere Christianity*. 1942. Reprint, London: HarperCollins, 2002.

Lossky, Vladimir. *In the Image and Likeness of God*. 1953. Reprint, Crestwood, NY: St. Vladimir's Seminary Press, 2001.

Lynch, M. "*Quid Pro Quo* Satisfaction? An Analysis and Response to Garry Williams on Penal Substitutionary Atonement and Definite Atonement." *Evangelical Quarterly* 89 (2018) 51–70.

Lyte, Henry Francis. "Praise, my soul, the King of Heaven." 1834.

MacIntyre, Alasdair. *After Virtue*. 3rd ed. London: Duckworth, 2007.

Marquand, David. *Mammon's Kingdom: An Essay on Britain, Now*. London: Allen Lane, 2014.

McIlroy, David. "Towards a Relational and Trinitarian Theology of Atonement." *Evangelical Quarterly* 80 (2008) 13–32.

Moore, George Foot. *Judaism in the First Centuries of the Christian Era*. Vol. 2: *The Age of the Tannaim*. Cambridge, MA: Harvard University Press, 1932.

Moltmann, Jürgen. *Experiences in Theology: Ways and Forms of Christian Theology*. Translated by Margaret Kohl. Gutersloh, Germany: Christian Kaiser, 2000.

Musseau, Craig, and Phyllis Musseau. "Forgiven." Brentwood, TN: Mercy/Vineyard Publishing, 1992.

Nalluri, Bharat, dir. *The Man Who Invented Christmas*. Toronto, Canada: Rhombus Films, 2017.

Ndundgane, Njongonkulu. "Seizing the New Millennium: Reshaping the World's Economy." In *Proclaim Liberty: Reflections on Theology and Debt*, edited by Susan Hawley, 25–34. London: Christian Aid, 1998.

Neff, Zama. "Meanwhile: For 15 Million in India, a Childhood of Slavery." *Human Rights Watch* January 31, 2003. https://www.hrw.org/news/2003/01/31/meanwhile-15-million-india-childhood-slavery.

Nietzsche, Friedrich. *On the Genealogy of Morality*. Translated by C. Diethe. Cambridge, UK: Cambridge University Press, 2006.

Nixon, Robin. "Fulfilling the Law: The Gospel and Acts." In *Law, Morality and the Bible*, edited by Bruce Kaye and Gordon Wenham, 53–71. Downers Grove, IL: InterVarsity, 1978.

BIBLIOGRAPHY

O'Donovan, Oliver. *Bonds of Imperfection: Christian Politics, Past and Present.* Grand Rapids, MI: Eerdmans, 2004.

———. *The Ways of Judgment.* Grand Rapids, MI: Eerdmans, 2005.

Orwell, George. *1984.* London: Secker & Warburg, 1949.

Owen, John. *The Death of Death in the Death of Christ: A Treatise in which the whole Controversy about Universal Redemption is Fully Discussed.* 1647. Reprint, London: Banner of Truth, 1959.

Paine, Thomas. *The Rights of Man.* 1791. In *Rights of Man, Common Sense, and Other Political Writings*, edited by Mark Philp, 83–331. Oxford: Oxford University Press, 1995.

Peterson, David G. *Where Wrath & Mercy Meet: Proclaiming the Atonement Today.* Carlisle, UK: Paternoster, 2001.

Peterson, Robert A. *Calvin and the Atonement.* Phillipsburg, NJ: P. & R. Publishing, 1983.

Pobee, John S. "The Ethics of Debt: A Theological Appraisal." In *Proclaim Liberty: Reflections on Theology and Debt*, edited by Susan Hawley, 65–72. London: Christian Aid, 1998.

Postman, Neil. *Amusing Ourselves to Death: Public Discourse in the Age of Show Business.* London: Penguin, 1985.

Redman, Matt. "I Will Offer Up My Life (This Thankful Heart)." Eastbourne, UK: ThankYou Music, 1994.

Richards, Noel. "Overwhelmed by Love." Eastbourne, UK: ThankYou Music, 1994.

Roberts, Alastair J., and Andrew Wilson. *Echoes of Exodus: Tracing Themes of Redemption through Scripture.* Wheaton, IL: Crossway, 2018.

Robinson, Julie Anne, dir. *Bridgerton.* Netflix, 2021.

Romanacce, George, et al. "Turn Your Eyes." Louisville, KY: Sovereign Grace Music, 2019.

Rowling, J. K. *Harry Potter and the Goblet of Fire.* London: Bloomsbury, 2001.

Rutledge, Fleming. *The Crucifixion: Understanding the Death of Jesus Christ.* Grand Rapids, MI: Eerdmans, 2015.

Scruton, Roger. "Regaining My Religion." https://matiane.wordpress.com/2020/05/06/regaining-my-religion-by-roger-scruton/.

Selby, Peter. *Grace and Mortgage: The Language of Faith and the Debt of the World.* London: Darton, Longman & Todd, 1997.

Smeaton, George. *The Apostles' Doctrine of the Atonement.* 1870. Reprint, Edinburgh: Banner of Truth, 1991.

Smith, J. K. A. *Derrida: Live Theory.* London: Continuum, 2005.

Soering, J. "'Justice, Justice Thou Shalt Pursue': Divine and Human Justice in a Correctional Context." *Justice Reflections* 16 (2007) 121.

Singh, Devin. "Sovereign Debt." *Journal of Religious Ethics* 46 (2018) 239–66.

Stimilli, Elettra. *Debt and Guilt: A Political Philosophy.* Translated by S. Porcelli. London: Bloomsbury, 2019.

———. *The Debt of the Living: Ascesis and Capitalism.* Translated by A. Bove. Albany, NY: State University of New York Press, 2017.

Sumner, D. "Theory and Metaphor in Calvin's Doctrine of the Atonement." *Princeton Theological Review* 13 (2007) 49–60.

BIBLIOGRAPHY

"Synod of Dort." https://prts.edu/wp-content/uploads/2016/12/Canons-of-Dort-with-Intro.pdf.

Ten Boom, Corrie. "I'm Still Learning To Forgive." Carmel, NY: Guideposts Magazine, 1972. http://storage.cloversites.com/citychurch/documents/Im%20Still%20Learning%20To%20Forgive.pdf.

Tomalin, Claire. *Charles Dickens: A Life*. London: Penguin, 2011.

Tomlin, Chris. "Amazing Grace (My Chains Are Gone)." Atlanta, GA: Sixsteps Music, 2006.

Torrance, T. F. *Atonement: The Person and Work of Christ*. Colorado Springs: IVP USA, 2009.

Vaus, Will. *Mere Theology: A Guide to the Thought of C. S. Lewis*. Leicester, UK: InterVarsity, 2004.

Vidu, Adonis. *Atonement, Law, and Justice: The Cross in Historical and Cultural Contexts*. Grand Rapids, MI: Baker Academic, 2014.

Watts, Isaac. "When I Survey The Wondrous Cross." 1707.

Webster, Douglas. *In Debt To Christ: A Study in the Meaning of the Cross*. London: Highway, 1957.

Welby, Justin. *Dethroning Mammon: Making Money Serve Grace*. London: Bloomsbury, 2016.

Wells, Paul. *Cross Words: The Biblical Doctrine of the Atonement*. Fearn, UK: Christian Focus, 2006.

"Westminster Confession of Faith, Chapter VIII." http://www.epcew.org.uk/resources/westminster-confession-of-faith/chapter-viii-of-christ-the-mediator.

Wetzel, J. "Snares of Truth: Augustine on Free Will and Predestination." In *Augustine and His Critics: Essays in Honour of Gerald Bonner*, edited by Robert Dodaro and George Lawless, 124–41. London: Routledge, 2002.

Williams, Garry J. "Penal Substitution: A Response to Recent Criticisms." *Journal of the Evangelical Theological Society* 50 (2007) 71–86.

Woznicki, Christopher. "The Coherence of Penal Substitution: An Edwardsean Defence." *Tyndale Bulletin* 70 (2019) 95–115.

Wright, Christopher J. H. *Human Rights: A Study in Biblical Themes*. Grove Booklets on Ethics 31. Cambridge, UK: Grove Books, 1979.

Wright, N. T. *The Climax of the Covenant: Christ and the Law in Pauline Theology*. Edinburgh: T. & T. Clark, 1991.

———. *The New Testament and the People of God*. Minneapolis: Fortress, 1992.

Subject Index

Abbott, Emma, 38–39
Abraham, 99
acceleration clauses, 83
Acts 10:38, 32
addiction, 22–23
"Amazing Grace" (Tomlin), 3
"Amazing Love" (Kendrick), 3–4
Anderson, Gary A., 7, 54
Anselm, archbishop of
    Canterbury, 31–32,
    118–19
Aristotle, 63
atonement, satisfaction theory
    of, 32
Augustine, 84
Boersma, Hans, 11, 12, 62–63,
    94
Bon Jovi, 38
bonded slavery, 39–40
Book of Exodus, 69
Brave New World (Huxley), 23
Bridgerton (Netflix series), 51
Broken April (Kadaré), 50–51
Brown, Henry "Box," 30
Burke, Edmund, 70–71
Burns, Robert, 10, 11
Calvin, John, 83
captivity, rescue from, 30
Carey, George, 72
certificate of indebtedness,
    89–90

Chandler, Paul and Rachel,
    18–19, 23
Charlton, Clive and Christine,
    115
cheirographon, 90
Chinnanan's story, 40–41
Christians Against Poverty, 7
2 Chronicles 34:33, 112
Chrysostom, John, 109
Colossians 1, 30
Colossians 2:13–14, 89–90
compounding, sacrifice and,
    46–48
1 Corinthians 7:21–23, 105
1 Corinthians 7:23, 65
1 Corinthians 15, 60
2 Corinthians 5:14–15, 107
covenant with people of Israel,
    106
covenant-faithfulness, 106
David Copperfield (Dickens),
    76–77
Debt (Graeber), 6
debt amnesties, 49
Debt and Guilt (Stimilli), 6, 23
debt bondage, 39–40
debt forgiveness, 6, 67–68,
    101–2. *See also* debt(s);
    forgiveness; Year of
    Jubilee
debt jubilees, 49

Subject Index

debt-cancellation, 103
Debtors Act, 80
debtors' prison, 74–80
debt(s)
   acceleration clause, 83
   acknowledging, 82–83
   cancellation of, 90
   as central paradigm of global economy, 6
   consequences of, 7
   of developing nations, 6
   Dickens's personal experiences with, 75–76
   dominating our lives, 5–7
   financial debts, 71–73
   forgiving debtors, 6, 67–68, 101–2
   gift-loans and, 103–4, 117
   to God, 69–70, 89–92
   good deeds outweighing bad, 24, 83
   of gratitude, 69–71, 80–81, 115
   of guilt. *See* guilt
   importance of, 5–6
   imposed on children of debtors, 71–73
   imprisonment for, 74–80
   incurred by sinning, 26
   interest-free loans, 115–16
   Jesus' death as payment of, 89–92
   of love, 106–8
   moral obligation and, 79
   national indebtedness, 71–73
   to parents, 70–71
   paying forward, 114–15, 116–17
   personal indebtedness, 73
   to previous generations, 70–71
   price paid for, 91–92
   recording, 90
   sin and, 7–8, 54, 114
   thankfulness and, 100–101
   as universal phenomenon, 7
   weighing us down, 2
debt-slavery, 39–41, 44, 49–50, 74–80, 95–96
Democratic Republic of the Congo (DRC), 71–72
Derrida, Jacques, 84–85
Dickens, Charles
   David Copperfield, 76–77
   on life for debtors, 76
   Little Dorrit, 79
   personal experiences with debt imprisonment, 75–76
   Pickwick Papers, 76, 77–78
Dudley-Smith, Timothy, 22
Edwards, Jonathan, 61
Egypt, judgment on, 97
English Court of Appeal, 80
Enmetena, 49
Ephesians 5:28, 107
eternal destiny of human beings, 24–25
Eubank, Nathan, 27, 103, 117–18
evil
   addiction to, 22–24
   fears of dystopian future and, 23
   power of, 20–22
Exodus 21:28–32, 48
exodus story
   impact on Israel's law, 45–52
   sacrifice and, 46–47
   as story of redemption, 42–44
Ezekiel 14, 26
family likeness, 108–9
financial debts, 71–73
financial metaphor, 70
the flesh, as power of evil, 20
"Forgiven" (Musseau), 4

Subject Index

forgiveness. *See also* debt forgiveness
  acceptance of truth as foundation for, 89
  certificate of indebtedness, 89–90
  consequences of, 101–2
  cost of, 84–88
  demands for, 85
  going beyond justice, 88
  guilt as precondition of, 88–89
  Jesus on, 87, 101–2
  The Lord's Prayer and, 14, 54, 103
  MacIntyre's condition of, 88–89
  in New Testament, 14–15
  obligation to, 102–3
  in Old Testament, 14
  redemption combined with, 92–93
  in songs and hymns, 4
  ungrateful servant parable and, 102–3
forgiveness metaphor, 14–16, 91–92. *See also* redemption metaphor
Forsyth, P. T., 20, 59–61, 82, 101, 104, 108
Founds, Rick, "Lord I Lift Your Name on High," 4
freed slaves, 44
Galatians 4, 64
gift-loans, 103–4, 117
Girard, René, 33
global financial crisis, 7
go'el, 42, 50
Grace and Mortgage (Selby), 6–7
Graeber, David, 6
gratitude
  debt of, 69–71, 80–81, 115
  replacing guilt, 115, 119

Great Commandments, 110, 111, 112–14
Great Commission, 111, 113–14
Gregory of Nazianus, 34–35, 63
Gregory of Nyssa, 32–33
guilt
  acknowledging, 82–83
  connection with debt, 14, 73–74
  as debts owed to God, 92
  gratitude replacing, 115, 119
  as key to spiritual health, 82
  measurement of, 114
  as precondition of forgiveness, 88–89
  redemption and, 45, 55
Harry Potter series (Rowling), 33
Hart, David Bentley, 91
Hays, Richard B., 65
"He Ransomed Me" (Johnston), 3
Heidelberg Catechism, 43–44
hôbâ, 54
holiness, 108–9
Holmes, Steve, 9, 27–28, 59, 94–95
Horner, Rob, 73, 82
Hosea, 54, 98
Hudson, Michael, 49
human economics, 118
Huxley, Aldous, 23
hymns. *See* songs and hymns
imprisonment for debt, 74–80
interest-free loans, 115–16
International Justice Mission (IJM), 40–41, 95–96
International Labour Organization, 40
Irenaeus, bishop of Lyons, 61–62, 117
Isaiah 41:14, 26
Isaiah 43:1, 44
Isaiah 44:22, 53–54

Subject Index

Isaiah 48:17, 65
Isaiah 50, 53
Isaiah 52, 53
Isaiah 59:20, 26
Isaiah 63:16, 52
Israelites, 42–43, 46–47, 69, 97–98, 99
James 1:15, 21
Jehoiakim, 113
Jeremiah, 113
Jeremiah 17:5, 25
Jesus
  baptism of, 62
  death and resurrection of. *See* Jesus' death
  on debt to God, 70
  on forgiveness, 87, 101–2
  on the Great Commandments, 112
  on the Great Commission, 113–14
  indebtedness to, 74
  as kinsman-redeemer, 94
  the Lord's Prayer and, 14, 103
  on money, 21, 104
  Nazareth Manifesto, 50
  as our surety, 60–62
  parables and, 8–9
  as Passover lamb, 45–46
  on paying it forward, 115–17
  predicting his resurrection, 57
  prodigal son parable, 81
  recapitulation of the human condition, 62
  Satan's attempt to claim rights over, 32–33
  in songs and hymns, 3–5
  unmerciful servant parable, 102–3
Jesus' death
  as cost of our salvation, 56–57
  as defining moment in human history, 12–13
  as forgiveness of debt to God, 89–92
  as our redemption, 56, 57, 97–98
  as ransom payment, 25–30, 34
Job, on God as eternal, 54
Job 33:24, 27–28
John 3:16, 34
1 John 4:20, 113
John the Baptist, 45
Johnston, Julia H., "He Ransomed Me," 3
Josiah, 112
Jubilee 2000 campaign, 6, 49
judgments against Jerusalem, 26
Kadaré, Ismail, 50–51
Keller, Tim, 84
Kendall, R. T., 100–101
Kendrick, Graham, "Amazing Love," 3–4
kidnappings, 18–19
2 Kings 22:2, 112
2 Kings 23:25, 112
king's ransom, 28–29
kinsman-redeemer, 50–52, 60
kipper, 42, 45
Kirkby, John, 7
The Last Supper, linked to Passover, 57–58
law of Moses, 39, 55, 75, 112, 117
Leopold, Duke of Austria, 28
levirate marriage, 51
Levites, 47
Leviticus 25, 52
Lewis, C. S., 13, 21–22, 57
The Lion, the Witch and the Wardrobe (Lewis), 21–22
Little Dorrit (Dickens), 79
living faithfully, 106
living freely, 105–8, 110

Subject Index

Living on a Prayer (Bon Jovi), 38
"Lord, for the Years" (Dudley-Smith), 22
"Lord I Lift Your Name on High" (Founds), 4
The Lord's Prayer, 14, 54, 103, 107
Lossky, Vladimir, 21
Luke 6:33–36, 104
Luke 12:13–21, 70
Luke 15:11–32, 81
Luke 18:18, 21
lutron, 27, 56. *See also* ransom
Lyte, Henry Francis, "Praise, my soul, the King of heaven," 4
MacIntyre, Alasdair, 88
marriage, 106–8
mass emancipations, 29
Matthew 20:19, 57
Matthew 20:28, 27
Matthew 25:31–46, 117
Matthew 28, 114
Medical Debt Relief Alliance (US), 104
metaphors
    capturing imagination, 16
    defined, 8
    of forgiveness. *See* forgiveness metaphor
    of God as shepherd, 11
    limitations of, 10–12
    as mini-stories, 8–9
    of money. *See* monetary metaphors
    in New Testament, 14–15
    in Old Testament, 14
    parables as extended, 8–9
    to picture the unimaginable, 12–13
    of ransom. *See* ransom metaphor
    of redemption. *See* redemption metaphor
    similes vs, 10–11
    unrecognized, 10
modern slavery. *See* debt-slavery
Moltmann, Jürgen, 102
monetary metaphors
    for atonement, 5
    biblical basis for, 14–16
    in songs and hymns, 3–5
    used in the Bible, 5
money, as object of worship, 21
Moore, George Foot, 82–83
Musseau, Craig and Phyllis, "Forgiven," 4
Narakalappa's story, 41
national indebtedness, 71–73
Nazareth Manifesto, 50
Neruja, Gianina Monica, 19
Nietzsche, Friedrich, 74, 92
1984 (Orwell), 23
On Cosmopolitanism and Forgiveness (Derrida), 84–85
Orwell, George, 23
"Overwhelmed by Love" (Richards), 4
Owen, John, 60
Owen, Rhiannon, 43
padah, 42, 45
Paine, Thomas, 80–81
parable(s)
    character of God in, 9
    as extended metaphors, 8–9
    of the prodigal son, 9, 81, 82, 88, 106
    of ungrateful servant, 102–3
Passover, linked to Last Supper, 57–58
Passover lamb, 45–46
patronage, 44
Paul (apostle), 55–56, 60, 64, 99, 105, 109–10
pawnbrokers, 37–38
1 Peter 1:18–19, 58

Subject Index

Pickwick Papers (Dickens), 76, 77–78
Pobee, John S., 69
poor in spirit, 82
Postman, Neil, 23
powers of evil. *See also* evil
    beyond our control, victims of, 22–24
    description of, 20–22
"Praise, my soul, the King of heaven" (Lyte), 4
prisoners of war, 29
prodigal son parable, 9, 81, 82, 88, 106
Proverbs 19:17, 117
Psalm 49:7–9, 26, 45
Psalm 74:2, 52
ransom
    Ananias's story, 111
    Chandler kidnapping, 18–19
    Jesus' death as payment of, 25–30, 34
    a king's ransom, 28–29
    mass emancipations and, 29
    in New Testament, 15
    paid to God, 34
    paid to the devil, 31–32
    payment of, 63–64
    prisoners of war and, 29
    redemption linked to, 45, 56
    Saeed kidnapping, 19
    setting others free from, 111–14
    in songs and hymns, 3
ransom metaphor. *See also* redemption metaphor
    captivity and, 26, 30, 35
    determining who is paid, 31–35
    emphasizing human beings as trapped, 25
    limits of, 34–35
    powers of evil and, 20
    problems with, 31–35
    salvation and, 24–25
    taken literally, 31
Ravensbrück concentration camp, 86
recapitulation, 61–62
reconciliation, 9, 81, 100
redemption
    cost of, 56–57
    defined, 50
    exodus story as story of, 42–44
    forgiveness combined with, 92–93
    as God buying back God's inheritance, 64–65
    of God's Son, 56, 57, 97–98
    implications of, 64–65
    inheritance and, 99–100
    of Israel, 97–98
    need for outside help, 38–39
    in New Testament, 15
    from oppression of men, 65
    from the pawnbroker, 37–38
    price paid for, 42–43, 57–60
    promise given to Abraham, 99
    ransom linked to, 45, 56
    from sin and death, 53–54, 55
    in songs and hymns, 3
    vendettas and, 50–51
redemption metaphor, 15–16, 36, 63–64, 92, 94. *See also* forgiveness metaphor; ransom metaphor
reparations, 68
Republic of Doyle (comedy-drama), 68–69
retribution, 114
Revelation 5:9, 58
Richard I "the Lionheart," 28–29
Richards, Noel, "Overwhelmed by Love," 4

Subject Index

Rights of Man (Paine), 80–81
Roberts, Alastair, 8, 55, 57–58, 105
Romans 3:21–25, 32
Romans 5:5, 88
Romans 5:12–21, 61
Romans 9:4–5, 99
Romans 13, 109–10
Rossman, Ted, 104
Rowling, J. K., *Harry Potter* series, 33
Ruth, 51–52
Rutledge, Fleming, 56
sacrifice, compounding and, 46–48
Sadeepan's story, 41
Saeed, Sahil, 19, 23
Saleem, Muhammad Zahid, 19
salvation, 24–25, 58
Scruton, Roger, 81
Selby, Peter, 6–7
self-centeredness, 20, 73
self-esteem, 82
self-interest, 117
self-restraint, 105
self-righteousness, 110
self-sacrifice, 9–10, 33
self-satisfaction, 22
Shallum, 113
similes, 10–11
Sin: A History (Anderson), 7, 54
sin(s)
    debt and, 7–8, 54, 114
    God suffering consequences of, 56–57
    incurs a debt, 114
    as pollution, 59
    as type of slavery, 55
slavery. *See also* debt-slavery
    Christ's death as redemption from, 63
    exile as return to, 53
    Israelites rescued from, 42
    as lawful, 66
    sin, as type of, 55
Smith, J. K. A., 84–85
songs and hymns
    forgiveness in, 4
    puncturing sense of self-satisfaction, 22–23
    ransom, 3
    redemption, 3
    as related to money, 3–5
South African Truth and Reconciliation Commission, 89
Stimilli, Elettra, 6, 23, 71
surety
    defined, 60
    Jesus as our, 60–63
    kinsman-redeemer and, 60
Synod of Dort, 58
Ten Boom, Corrie, 86–88
Ten Commandments, 69, 70, 105–6. *See also* Great Commandments
thankfulness, 100–101
1 Timothy 6:10, 21
tithe/tithing, 101
Titus 2:13–14, 109
Titus 2:14, 65
Tomalin, Claire, 75–76, 79
Tomlin, Chris, "Amazing Grace," 3
Torrance, T. F., 26, 32, 42, 45, 96–97, 99
Tutu, Desmond, 84, 89
Ugandan Christian Lawyers Fraternity (UCLF), 111
ungrateful servant parable, 102–3
vendettas, 50–51
Watts, Isaac, 46
Webster, Douglas, 29, 92, 101
Westminster Confession of Faith, 100
Wilson, Andrew, 8, 55, 57–58, 105

Wordsworth, William, 10, 11
World Bank, 71–72
world's value system, as power
    of evil, 20

Wright, N. T., 8–9, 97
Year of Jubilee, 48–50, 52, 68.
    See also Jubilee 2000
    campaign

Scripture Index

OLD TESTAMENT

Genesis
6:6–7	30
22	46
34	63
50:17	14

Exodus
1	43
1:22	97
2:23	42
4:22	97
6:6	45, 64
7:14–24	42
10:21–29	42
11	42
12	42
12:12	42
13:1–2	47
13:3	42
13:14	42
13:14–16	47
15:13	45
20:2	42, 69, 106
21:28–32	48
21:29	48
21:30	48
22:25	116
22:26	39
23:19	46
23:21	14
30:12	14
32:10	30
34:9	14

Leviticus
6:7	14
19:20	27
23:10	46
25	39, 45
25:7–49	75
25:8–55	48
25:36–37	116
25:42	43
25:48	52
25:51–52	27
25:54–55	52
25:55	43
27	14
27:29	14, 48

Numbers
3:11–13	47
3:12	27
3:44–51	47
3:46–51	27
12:10	10

Numbers (*continued*)

18:15	27
18:16	47
35:19	50
35:21–32	14
35:31–32	48

Deuteronomy

	97
5:6	42
6:12	42
7:8	30, 42
8:14	42
9:26	64
13:5	42
15:15	42
18:4	46
21:23	56
23:19	116
24:12	39
24:18	42
25:5–9	51

Joshua

24:17	42

Judges

6:8	42

Ruth

1	51
3:10–13	51
4:5	52

2 Samuel

7:23	64

2 Kings

5:27	10
22:2	112
22:5	112
23:3	112
23:25	112

1 Chronicles

17:2	64

2 Chronicles

34:33	112
35:18	112

Nehemiah

5:10	116

Job

7:20	14
19:25–27	54
33	45
33:24	27, 28
33:27	27

Psalms

15:5	116
19:12	14
23	10
24:22	54
25:1	14
32	89
32:1	14
32:5	89
34:22	52
44:26	54
49	45
49:5–9	28
49:7–9	26, 45
49:15	28, 54
51:7	10
69:18	54
74:2	52, 64
77:15	64
78:42	64
79:9	14
103:4	54
106:10–12	64

Scripture Index

119:134	54, 65
130:7–8	54
130:7b–8	54

Proverbs

19:17	117
28:8	116

Isaiah

1:18	10
1:27	65
6:3	70
41:14	26
43:1	44
44:6	52
44:22	53
45:13	27
48:17	65
50	53
50:1	53
52:3	53
52:5	53
54:5	52
59:20	26
61	75
62:12	65
63:16	52

Jeremiah

17:5	25
18:14	10
22:13–17	113

Ezekiel

14	26
14:16	26
18:8	116

Hosea

11:1–4	98
13:14–16	54

ANCIENT JEWISH WRITERS

Josephus	103

NEW TESTAMENT

Matthew

Matthew	101
5	85
5:3	82
5:43–48	117
6:12	14, 54, 103, 107
16:24–26	118
18	102
18:23–35	14, 69, 102, 103
19:24	21
19:29	118
20:19	57
20:28	15, 27
22:37–38	112
22:37–40	114
22:39	112
23:37	98
25:31–46	117
28	95, 113

Mark

10:45	26

Luke

4	50
4:18–19	50
6:33–36	104
11:4	14, 107
11:13	116
12:13–21	70
15:11–32	81

Scripture Index

Luke (*continued*)
15:16	9
15:17	82
15:21	81
15:29	81
18:18	21
21:28	15
22:20	57

John
1:3	74
1:29	45, 74
3:16	34

Acts
10:38	32

Romans
1:18–32	55
2	55
3:20	55
3:21–25	32
3:21–26	55
3:24	15
4:7	15
4:25	61
5:5	88
5:9	116
5:10	116
5:12–21	61
5:15–17	117
6:1–14	55
6:15–23	55
6:23	55
7:1–25	55
8	109
8:1	109
8:1–11	55
8:2	109
8:4	109
8:12–17	55
8:18–25	55
8:23	15
8:26–39	55
9:4–5	99
13	109
13:8	107

1 Corinthians — 65
1:30	15, 64
5:7	46
6:19	105
7	105
7:21–23	105
7:23	65
11:25	57
13	108
15	60
15:20	60
15:22	60
15:23	60
15:25–26	60

2 Corinthians
1:22	96
2	15
3:9	117
5:14–15	107

Galatians
3	99
3:13	56, 99
3:14	99
4	64
4:5	64
4:6	64

Ephesians
1:7	15, 92
1:13–14	96
1:14	15
1:18	118
4:30	15, 96
5:28	107

Scripture Index

Philippians

4:6	100

Colossians

1	30
1:13	30
1:14	15, 92
2:12	96
2:13–14 NASB	89–90
3:11–12	96
3:13	15

1 Timothy

2:6	15, 26
6:8	116
6:10	21

Titus

2:13–14	109
2:14	65

Hebrews

8:12	15
9	16
9:12	16, 58
9:15	15, 16
9:22	15
10:18	15
11:6	107

James

1:15	21
1:17	70

1 Peter

1:18–19	58

1 John

	113
1:9	15
2:12	15
4:20	113

Revelation

4:8	70
5:9	58
7:17	90
21:4	90

Romans

3:21–25	32

EARLY CHRISTIAN WRITINGS

Anonymous
Incomplete Work on Matthew, Homily 4   62

Augustine
Ad Simplicianum   84, 84n21

Chrysostom, John
Homilies on Romans 13   109, 109n17

Gregory of Nazianus   34–35, 63
"Dogmatic Poems"
    I.viii.65–69   34n13
Oration 45
    22   35n14

Gregory of Nyssa   32, 63
The Great Catechism   63n26

Irenaeus   62, 117
Against Heresies
    IV.18.6   117n19
    V.17.2   62n24

www.ingramcontent.com/pod-product-compliance
Lightning Source LLC
Chambersburg PA
CBHW072148160426
43197CB00012B/2301